Tree of Dreams

A SPIRIT WOMAN'S
VISION OF TRANSITION
AND CHANGE

Jeremy P. Tarcher/Putnam
a member of Penguin Putnam Inc. / New York

Tree of Dreams

Lynn Andrews

Most Tarcher/Putnam books are available at special quantity discounts
for bulk purchases for sales promotions, premiums, fund-raising, and
educational needs. Special books or book excerpts also can be created
to fit specific needs. For details, write Putnam Special Markets,
375 Hudson Street, New York, NY 10014.

Jeremy P. Tarcher/Putnam
a member of
Penguin Putnam Inc.
375 Hudson Street
New York, NY 10014
www.penguinputnam.com

First paperback edition 2003

The Library of Congress Catalogued the hardcover as follows:

Andrews, Lynn
Tree of dreams : a spirit woman's vision of
transition and change /
Lynn Andrews.
p.   cm.
ISBN 1-58542-129-4
1. Andrews, Lynn.   2. Shamanism—Miscellanea.   3. Indians
of North America—Religion—Miscellanea.   I. Title.
BP610 .A54175   2001   2001027738
299'.93—dc21

ISBN 1-58542-215-0 (Paperback edition)

Printed in the United States of America

1   3   5   7   9   10   8   6   4   2

Book design by Jennifer Ann Daddio

▲ ▲ ▲

IN APPRECIATION . . .

To Al Lowman for his extraordinary insights.

To Kathy Duckworth for her friendship and endurance.

Particularly to my editor, Laura Shepherd,
for her clarity and inspiration.

And as always, to my dear teachers,
the women of the Sisterhood of the Shields,
and all of the beings of light who surround me.

▲ ▲ ▲

This book is dedicated to the circle

of life and the divine wisdom within

the process of death and life.

Contents

Time When the Leaves Turn Dark Green

Time When the Trees Blossom

Time When the Leaves Turn Gold

Tree Blossoms Fall and the Leaves Are Crimson

Crimson, Gold, and Orange . . . the Leaves Begin to Fall

All the Leaves Have Fallen and the Trees Begin Their Winter Dreams

▲ ▲ ▲

Love and death are the two gifts that we pass on,

and usually they are passed on unopened.

—RAINER MARIA RILKE

Preface

I began to tell my story twenty years ago. Except for changes in names and locations, it is true.

In the north of Manitoba, Canada, nestled under quaking poplar trees along Dead Man's Creek, are two old log cabins a short distance apart. Agnes Whistling Elk and Ruby Plenty Chiefs live there at certain times of the year. They are elder women of power who "know how." They are Native American women who have memorized and handed down to their apprentices and family women a system of universal knowledge that has been held pure and secret for thousands of years. There are kindlings of truth in their voices, and the dry gold of their words has settled on my tongue and changed my life forever.

"Your people live on borrowed knowledge," Agnes Whistling Elk said to me when we first met. "If you become my apprentice, you will learn through experience."

And that was the beginning. Indeed, I have gained priceless

knowledge from Agnes and the forty-three other native women of the Sisterhood of the Shields. And every few years I have felt compelled to share that wisdom and experience with my own students and readership. I have learned from them, and I have shared the experiences they have taught me.

This is not a how-to book in which the steps are carefully explained. Everything of value that I have learned from my teachers has come to me in a most unusual way. My teachers show how through story and experience—pieces that at first seem unrelated. But yet, when all the pieces or fragments of these experiences are brought together, they form a whole. All the little pieces of life, seemingly unimportant, gradually lead to a realization of truth. It is rarely a singular event that leads us to truth. Instead, it's rather like a circle made up of small experiences. Power is found in the center. You must circle power in order to find it and bring yourself to the center, to the essence of what you are trying to learn.

Now as I enter the second half of my life, perhaps the greatest challenge lies ahead. The transition to "elderhood" is a mysterious and sometimes frightening passage, and it presses on despite my attempts to shut it out or understand its process. As I relate in the chapters that follow, the experience of facing mortality has enriched me and has also taken me to the highest point of my spiritual exploration. Perhaps you too are in the midst of transition or at the edge of loss. If so, I offer my experience as witness to the magnificent life-and-death process of my friends who are elder Native American women, surrealistically compared to the lives of my Western friends and the death of my stepfather in the modern surroundings of an urban hospital. These two passages, coming as they did upon the heels of one another, forged an awesome lesson for me about awareness.

Red Dog, an old adversary in my books and life, has also seemingly risen from the dead and again interrupts my sense of well-being with his sorcery and fascination for eternal life. His reappearance challenges my ideals about death, rebirth, and mortality. This story then has been woven out of both the threads of our urban lives and the magical existence of another way of seeing reality that coincides with it.

My mentors, Agnes Whistling Elk, Ruby Plenty Chiefs, and Spider Woman are old women by any standards, but they have transformed physical frailty into wisdom and strength so that you might mistake them for agile young women. However, they teach me in the old way. They play tricks and behave outrageously. They are filled with humor and possess a sharp edge of wisdom that can cut to the bone. Their lessons are not always obvious, and as is so often the case with anything meaningful, they are sometimes difficult or painful to learn. I have become a teacher now myself, but I still work with these women, as the process of learning in this life is never over. Often I play the fool to them, as well they know, because my vulnerability allows their truth to be complete. We play, we learn, and we grow, as you will see.

Lynn Andrews
Santa Fe, New Mexico

Introduction

"I want my life to be filled with magic," I said.

Ruby Plenty Chiefs looked at me with a slight air of contempt that didn't fill me with much confidence, and I told her so. We sat on her wooden porch in Canada, tying herbs into bundles to dry.

"Ruby, I need to explain how I got here, not for a teaching as much as for people to know where I came from."

"Well, where did you come from?" Ruby asked.

Ruby is an old Indian woman with long salt-and-pepper braids that brush against her red plaid shirt. She wears a beautiful beaded deer shield and jean skirt. She empties her moccasin of sand and watches me with her blue-gray eyes. She was blinded as a young girl by white surveyors after they had raped her, but she has learned through years of practice and the teachings of the Sisterhood to see better than most anyone. She uses sound, smell, and her heightened sensitivity to air pressure. Ruby can see with "spirit" eyes by entering the astral field at will. This is part of the process we call "dreaming," and it can be learned through meditation, knowledge, and practice with a teacher.

"Well," I began, "I was living in Beverly Hills, and I had been searching for a teacher all of my life, but especially in the ten years before I met you and Agnes," I said. "I felt that I needed to learn from another woman—someone who would understand my female nature. Even though I loved and honored and respected the male teachers who had inspired me in many ways, I still wanted to find a woman teacher who could help me to develop and understand my special abilities."

"What were those?" Ruby asked, standing up and walking into her cabin to hang some of her herbs from nails that were stuck in a rafter in her one room. She hung them above the bed, came back, and said, "You know, I love the smell of that sweet grass. I always hang it above the bed to bless my sleep." She winked at me and sat down to twist some braids of sweet grass into long ropes.

"I could see lights around people, Ruby. You know this. I could always see aspects of their strengths and weaknesses."

"What did you see when you first saw me?" Ruby asked.

"Besides the fact that you scared me half to death as you stood over that freshly killed deer, brandishing that knife the way you did as you came toward me? I had been searching the wilderness for you. I had never seen you before, but when I did, I knew I was home. I would have done anything you asked. You were formidable with your shining eyes and your knife. But I could sense your wisdom and your power. Your voice was strange and melodic as you ordered me to take the knife and skin the deer before the sun set. You knew how desperately hard that was for me to do something so foreign, but I knew I had to do it or you would send me away. I must tell you, Ruby, it was both a marvelous and a horrible experience."

"I was only testing you," she said. "I wanted to see what you were made of. I thought surely you were like every other *wasishu* around here."

"Oh, thanks," I said.

She laughed and poked me with her elbow.

"So go on, what did you see?"

"I saw something very unusual, Ruby," I said, looking at her through my left eye more than my right. "I saw jagged shards of light around you. It took me aback and it frightened me. I'd never seen anything like it."

"What do you mean, 'shards of light'?"

"Well, it was strange. The light around you enveloped you to the point where you disappeared into it."

"Yeah, go on."

"That was about it. Isn't that enough?"

"No, there was more."

"What do you mean there was more?"

"I was showing you something," she said, "and I felt sure that you could see it. That was a good sign."

I sat back in my rickety wooden chair, trying not to collapse it onto the floor, and thought for a while.

"There *was* more," I added. "I noticed that instead of the light being pure white, like I'm used to seeing most of the time, I saw shadowed, crystalline edges. Does that make any sense?"

"Yes."

"What was that? What were you doing? I've never seen you do that again."

"Since then, there has been no reason for me to do that."

"What do you mean, Ruby, 'to do that'?"

"Sometimes, as you well know, you show people a form. You show people an aspect of your sacredness to see if they can see it."

"Why would you do that?" I asked.

"I do that because I need to know where people are. I need to know what they are mixed up with."

"Mixed up with?"

"If you look at a plant . . ."

She held up some herbs that we had picked earlier that morning, some mustard-flower herbs.

"These plants, when they are growing, are not mixed up with anything. They aren't trying to become a rose or the poplar tree that is sheltering them, or anything else. They're just what they are. Now people—we get confused. We get mixed up with things, and when we do, we tend to lose our way. We get all wrapped around something, like a vine, and we think it's the truth. We think it's the truth because it's bigger than we are, maybe we think it's better than we are, because we're not worthy. It's like a parasite living off of something. Instead of two trees standing in the same shade, we become interlocked, interwoven with ideas that don't belong to us, teachings that don't belong to us."

She observed me for a while as I sat and thought about her words carefully.

"But to learn, Ruby," I said, "sometimes you have to wrap around something to learn it, don't you?"

"There are two ways to wrap around something. One way is to suck it dry like a parasite that lives off of its host until the host is dead. And then what does it have? Nothing. It usually dies. That's one way. The other way is to be of service."

"What's the difference?" I asked, taking several bundles of herbs and preparing them to be hung. I sniffed one for a long time—rosemary—breathing in deeply and watching the light play across the old woman's face. She was so beautiful that she took my breath away. I was thankful to be in her presence.

"Service," Ruby said, leaning forward a bit to make sure I was listening carefully, "is not servitude. As you become an apprentice, you begin to anticipate what I need, and in this way you yourself become the teacher. You think about what I told you, and about everything you've learned so far, so that you can be of service to me. In that way you learn what the teacher is made of. And when you learn that, then you've learned the lesson. Then I am free and you are free, and we walk away from each other in love, in complete autonomy and freedom, but in complete service to one another. There is a community, in a sense, between us. We love each other, we care for each other, but we are free from each other. You are not dependent on my life force, little wolf, and I am not dependent on yours. Service is how you begin to understand personal power, how you begin to understand the teacher, the guru, the great one, the wise one that teaches you. You have to become them and walk in their path. You serve as an apprentice, but as you serve, you do not lose yourself. You are motivated from a place of passion within your own unique life. We call this making an act of power. During our years together, why do you think we talk about acts of power so much? Because in an act of power, you create the mirrors that become your teacher. When you act or make choices—a husband, a profession—you create mirrors in which you see yourself."

There was a noise behind me. I swiveled my head around to find our friend Agnes standing there, hands on her hips.

"Well," she said, "act of power? What . . . are we going back to basics here?"

We laughed. Agnes grinned at me.

"What's up?" she said.

"Well, I'm trying to figure out how to talk about my beginnings as an apprentice, Agnes. How did I get here? What made me come?"

"Why didn't you ask me?" she said.

"I would have if you'd been here."

"I could have told you. It was destiny. Simple. It was written. It has been written throughout the ages that you would come, and you did. We were expecting you. We waited a long time, but we knew of your coming."

"I know now that this is my destiny, and I know that you sent me a kind of invitation by sending me a photograph of the marriage basket. When I saw that picture, the vision of the beautiful marriage basket began to obsess me. I had never seen a basket like it. When I went back to the art gallery to buy the photo, the owner said it didn't exist and I had been seeing things. Then you appeared in my dreams, handing the basket to me, and I followed those dreams."

"That's right," Agnes said. "What's so complicated about that?"

"A lot of people may not understand that."

"Okay," Agnes said, squatting down on the ground and drawing a circle. "Let's just see what it looks like on the sacred circle, as we always do. Remember? ABCs," she said.

"All right, Agnes, yes," and I squatted down next to her in the dirt. Ruby continued with her herb bundles.

"You in the south—that represents the physical. You wanted to know what was happening to you physically. You were puzzled by the fact that you could see into people. Right, Lynn?" Agnes began to sign with her hands as she spoke.

"Yes, Agnes."

"You could see into people," she repeated. "You knew if something was wrong or something was right. You knew when they lied to you. You could see their illnesses. You could see their power— you sensed it. You followed that vision and went in search of a teacher." She took a handful of earth and let it drift on the wind.

"They were from the East. They were from Africa. They were

from all over the world. You loved the teachers you found, but because you are a woman, you knew that you had to learn from a woman who was of this time and of this soil. You were looking for your spiritual home."

"Yes."

"Black wolf, then what did you do? You saw a representation of us physically, a symbol of us, which was the picture of the marriage basket in the gallery opening on La Cienega those many years ago at a Stieglitz exhibit! How interesting, isn't it, that now you find yourself at Ghost Ranch where Georgia O'Keeffe, the wife of Stieglitz, lived? Well, it makes perfect sense. You followed the dream. In the dream we came and we gathered you, we enticed you, we frightened you, we woke you up." She put her hand on my solar plexus. "That's what we did. We woke you up to your dreaming. You had a pretty good dream body, even in those days. You've always been a dreamer, but we've been in your dreams much more than you remember."

"You have?" I asked, surprised.

"Oh, yes."

"Well, in those days the dream felt more like a nightmare," I said.

"What do you mean, a nightmare?" Agnes asked.

"I'd see you holding this basket out to me and calling to me, saying, 'It is time.' I didn't know what that meant."

"But somehow you did know what it meant," Ruby interrupted.

"In a way I did. I was filled with an obsessive need to uncover the mystery of our dreaming together. I didn't know who you were, and I didn't know why you were there, but I had to find out."

"Actually," Ruby said, "you've wanted to know your whole life, even when you were a little girl. You spent part of your life on a little ranch in eastern Washington, and your friends were all Native

American. Remember that? Remember the basket you saw in the morning light in Beverly's cabin? You were spending the night, and you saw that basket. You got up early in the morning, and you went and touched it. Remember how everybody was so mad at you?"

"Yes," I said, "I was absolutely terrified."

"The basket was sacred. It symbolized the balance between male and female, and it spoke to you. You were only six years old, and you've never forgotten that—you just thought you had."

I was stunned. I had never heard Agnes and Ruby talk about that moment.

"You mean to tell me that experience had something to do with the Sisterhood?" I said.

"Yes, it did. It was the beginning of your journey to truth, to meaning. Your whole life has been a vision quest. Remember how you used to get on your horse at dawn and ride until sunset every day? You were very young to be allowed to go out into the wilderness all day long. And yes, you rode with your Indian friend, but you were oftentimes all by yourself. Your father allowed you to do that, and that was good, because he knew that you needed it and were capable of taking care of yourself. All of those years you were forming a dialogue with nature and with the divine."

Agnes took hold of my hand and looked into my eyes.

"Why do you think you chose to go to Catholic schools?" she asked. "You're not Catholic."

"I wanted to take music lessons, and I wanted to go into the chapel and pray."

"That's right," she said. "That was your destiny—to pray. Do you think the Great Spirit didn't hear you?"

"I know that somebody heard me."

"Yes, they did, and they answered your prayers. They spoke of your coming to us, as it was written. You were destined to take our teachings out into the world. It was what you were meant to do. All of the other things—your beautiful daughter, your marriages, your friends, the people you know—all of them are mirrors you've created. But mostly, you wanted to pray."

"Yes," I said. Tears stung my eyelids as I realized the meaningful connection that had been formed so early in my life.

"I used to get in trouble. I would ask the nuns how I could love a god that I was told to fear. They would tell me to go pray in the chapel. I even wanted to be a nun at one point."

"That would have been pretty funny," they both said at once, and I laughed.

"That's your interest in Mary Magdalene. That's your interest in so many other aspects of different religions in the world. But remember, in your heart and soul, you were like a Black Madonna."

"How do you mean?"

"You were the unrecognized one," Agnes continued, taking up a stick and beginning to whittle with her buck knife. "You were the one who could not be seen. Even though your father, a brilliant, educated man, loved you, he also abused you. You couldn't trust him. And your mother, she was full of dreams that were unrealized. She couldn't speak of them to you, so a gulf formed between you that was crossed only in later years. You were alone. You couldn't speak to her. You couldn't speak to him. You didn't trust him, you could say only what he wanted to hear. You grew up an only child of divorced parents. You lived with your mother during school years, which were difficult, because you were pretending that you were somebody you weren't. You were popular. You were a cheerleader. You studied. You did all those things. But you were alone and you were depressed because nobody knew who you were, and you didn't feel worthy. This is how many women feel today. In a sense, this explains your fascination with Mary Magdalene or the Black Madonna. She was you and you were her in a symbolic way. Why did you pick women to work with? Because you're a woman. You needed us. You still do. You need us to understand your place in the world. It's not an easy road. This path is a difficult one, but you chose it. You've only yourself to blame," she said, smiling.

"Here in the north . . ." Agnes brought me back now to the sacred wheel that she had scratched into the earth. "Here in the north is spirit. Who brought prayer to the people but White Buffalo Woman? White Buffalo Woman symbolically is like Mary Magdalene. She is the one who brought sacred balance to the male-oriented society and taught prayer. Prayer is not only female; it's male, too. But at the time, you needed the female.

"Now woman is becoming visible, but if you are going to be visible, little wolf, do not be visible like a man. Or, if you have to be visible like a man, please be a nice one."

They laughed uproariously at Agnes's joke. I sat and stared at them both, seeing once again the link of all living things in this life. We all live together. We all sing the same song. We all are in search of power.

"My destiny was before me. Even as a little girl in eastern Washington, as I rode my horse, Sugar, along a dirt road and smelled the grass and trees after a rain, I used to wonder what my destiny was. I knew my destiny was with God, because I would talk with God all day and all night long. I kept asking him what I was supposed to be doing on this earth. I knew I was much different than everybody at school because I could see things. I just tried to fit in the best that I could, but I was a sad outsider. I would make bundles of my dreams and bury them, hoping to find them someday realized. I would climb up in the apple tree and write, which made me feel better. I would write stories about little pinto horses, Spice and Spunk, but I found it hard to write the endings of stories. I could almost never do it."

"And," Agnes said, "that's why we made it so difficult for you.

We made you so angry, so you would have to go write the first book about our work together."

"Our work together . . ." I said. "Yes, our work together," I repeated. "You threw me out. Do you remember that?" I asked. I got angry all over again right on the spot.

"Yes, you were angry as all get out. We asked you to come up and join us on the reserve for two years. You rented out your house, your daughter was in school, and up you came. You were very poor in those days. You used all the money you had to get up here. You had just enough money to get back to California, and we knew it."

"Why? Explain to me again why you did that. Oh, you made me so mad!"

"We wanted to get you where it hurt," Agnes said. "You needed a lot of props. You needed your telephone, your friends, your books. You needed your comfortable little house in Beverly Hills. You needed all those things to keep you asleep."

"What do you mean, to keep me asleep? I was very awake."

"No, you weren't."

"Yes, I was."

"Well, no you weren't," Agnes said. "And that's why it hurt so much."

I was devastated. I remember running down the hill to Agnes's cabin with my bag, so excited to be with my teachers. I had rented out my house with an ironclad lease. Everything was in order, except for one small thing. There was Agnes sitting by the fire, next to her cabin. She turned very cold eyes on me and asked me what I was doing there.

"But Agnes," I had said, "I'm so excited to see you. I'm so thrilled to be here in your presence for two years."

She had said, "But what are you talking about? You aren't Indian. You don't belong here."

I looked at her in horror and tears began slipping down my cheeks. "I thought you wanted me here."

She stood up dramatically and said, with her hands and fingers spread above her, "Let the eagles fly. Take what you have learned about the ancient and sacred power of our ways to your people."

I stood staring at her, speechless for a moment. "But you have asked me not to tell anyone about you. Except for a couple of people, no one knows that you exist. Take it to my people? What, on a soap box?"

"No," she said, very firmly and with an attitude of absolute resolve. "No, you write the first of many books about our life and work together."

"Write a book?" I said.

"Yes, a book."

"A book."

"Yes." And then Agnes looked at me and said, "Beginning, middle, *and* end."

All the women in the Sisterhood knew that I was a writer. All of my life I had been a writer. But I was an author who was not writing. Fortunately, I had managed to jot down practically everything they had told me. I had described our ceremonies. I had written these things on pieces of paper, on pieces of bark, on my clothing, on anything I could find. Ruby always said I would remember when I needed to, but I didn't trust that. For the first time, the words came quickly and easily.

Back in those days when they rejected me, I had been filled with so much anger. I looked at Agnes and said, "What am I doing here? How could I have I been so stupid to think that you would lead me to a path of heart or knowledge! You've tricked me! How could you? I have no place to go. I have no money. What am I going to do? How can I possibly write anything under these conditions?"

I was crying. I was so angry, I wanted to strike her. Instead, I sat down on the ground on my suitcase and stared at her in absolute disbelief.

I remember those days still, sometimes with a smile and sometimes with horror at the position they had put me in, because at that time, I truly did not know where to go. My friends knew nothing about these women. Who would have believed me? Was I supposed to go back and stay with some kind friend while I wrote my life's work? In despair, I ended up renting a small cabin north of Santa Barbara in a place named Paradise, which was truly a misnomer. It took me two years to pull my notes together and gather my senses. I realized that however long the journey, Agnes and Ruby would not summon me again with their dreams. They would no longer visit me in this way. In the past, Agnes and Ruby would work with me when I slept at night. They came to me, and I went out of my body. I worked with them, and they taught me. But now that was cut off as well. When Agnes threw me out of the cabin that night, she told me that she would not dream me, that none of them would dream me. It would be as if they were gone until I finished the book and returned. For more than two years, they were only a memory to me.

So I wrote, and during that time, I went through my shaman death, which is akin to an ego death. Many people go through this in life. You lose your sense of self, or identity. Through difficult times, you struggle to find your balance. Then, if you are lucky, you feel reborn into a new identity that is much more aware and profound. Agnes called this period of struggle "the weirds." There is no question that you redefine your own sanity. My shaman death occurred because I was so afraid to finish first, to write something worthwhile, to be noticed. As an abused child you learn to blend in to the background, because if you are noticed, you often get hit. Finding the courage to step out on my own was a most extraordinary experience. I became terribly confused. Until they threw me out, I thought I was accomplished, because I had done many things in my life. I had been to college and started companies and made films and traveled all over the world. But when it came to writing my book, I was undisciplined and unorganized. My mind would cloud over. I couldn't even remember what I had done, where, when, or how. I had to clear my mind and find a way to get past the part of myself that would sabotage my effort. It became very clear to me early on why Agnes had made me so angry. She wanted to give me the strength to do what I needed to do. She had awakened my will, and my will was aflame. I was going to finish this and show them. That's what got me through my shaman death.

Oddly enough, I awoke one morning in my little single-walled cabin and opened my eyes to discover that the cabin was filled with light. I saw the Buddha walk through the door. Why the Buddha? I couldn't imagine, but there he was. He was smiling, and he asked the strangest question. "Where's the Buddha? I'm looking for the Buddha."

"You're looking for the Buddha?" I said, perplexed. "But you are the Buddha. Why would you be looking for yourself?"

"Maybe the Buddha is in the kitchen." He went off to the little kitchen, came back out, and said, "Well, the Buddha isn't there. Maybe he's in the living room."

"Why are you looking for what's in front of your nose? You are the Buddha!"

He turned around and looked at me. Smiling, he said, "That's right." Then he said, laughing, "Maybe I'll find the Buddha down by the river."

He walked out the door of my cabin and disappeared. I thought about that vision for weeks and finally realized that we are all searching for God when we need look no further than inside ourselves. We are home, but we just don't know it. At that point I started to laugh, and I kept laughing for three days. That was a life-changing experience if ever there was one. The laughing Buddha stood right before me. He was laughing at me and with me in my search for myself. When I understood the simplicity of what he was saying, my whole belief system, my knowledge of what was true and not true, went through a major meltdown. I moved into humor—pure, sacred humor. And I couldn't stop laughing.

As the months ticked by, I befriended a medicine man who lived nearby my cabin. I believe he came there to watch over me. We walked along the river and talked. I hung onto my sanity by a very thin thread. At times I nearly lost it altogether, but I never lost the reality that I was living in. I think there comes a moment when you can choose madness or not. I chose to stay in the reality that I inhabit, although this may have been the more difficult choice. Things had changed forever. Many teachers and mystics have written about that shift. They speak of vision turning upside down before it turns over. Your personality doesn't change, but who you are does. Your motivations change and your ability to see the sacred dream, as my teachers call it, or the illusion of life, shifts, and you see life differently than you ever saw it before. In a sense, you become a contradiction.

Someone may ask you one day what you feel and what you believe about certain aspects of truth. You may make a comment that is completely and totally contradicted the next day when they ask you something else. How and why does that happen? It happens because what we often see in life is an illusion. But we don't know how to move beyond it until we reach the place my teachers call power, personal power. In other religious beliefs this place may be called God or samadhi or enlightenment. We get glimpses of the face of God. It's as if the lens of the eye of perception opens, and we see truth for a moment. Of course, that vision always closes, because it's more than we can stand for very long. But from that point on, although we continue to live in that illusion, we find our way home, taking those empty spaces of our being and lifting them up to God for illumination and understanding.

On my path I went through the anguish of my shaman death, but I lived through it. Now I am no longer afraid of death. I have experienced a kind of death that brought me to the other side of terror, to the peace of creativity. I found the other side of the chasm, and I wrote *Medicine Woman* from my heart and my soul, wanting other people to see my frailties for the first time in my life, wanting other people to experience the terrors, the joys, and the bliss that I had experienced through my teachers. I wanted my readers to find the courage to follow their dreams. I thought the telling of my journey might help them to see themselves or find a teacher. My teachers are very unusual. Being with them is not like being in a monastery or meditating. It is not like being in school where you read a book and take a test. They teach through experience. They never teach borrowed knowledge. They teach from their experience and the mirrors that are provided by this life of choices. They feel this is the way we learn to understand our consciousness most deeply. Because I have experienced teaching and truth this way, I employ this method in my school and in my books. I try to lead the apprentice along the journey with me, a journey that I have walked ahead of them. Perhaps I pick up the trail for them. It depends. Everyone is different. Everyone needs to learn something different. I do not presume to know what someone else needs to learn, but I can see and I have been trained to open my sacred vision and *See*, with a capital *S*. What does that mean? It means that I see beyond what is ordinarily seen with ordinary eyes. I can see spirit and how consciousness is manifesting self.

Once I was sitting in circle with my teachers, and I said to Twin Dreamers, one of the women, "How do I explain power to someone? How do I explain what this means, this incredible experience of love that I have just had?"

She said, "Describe the experience only, because if you try to describe what power is, you lose the depth of it. Power cannot possibly come to you or to the person you are speaking with by describing it. Then you will surely lose it. You can only circle it and take someone to the center, and then they have to find it for themselves. They have to take that mirror and peer inside and grow from the consciousness that is reflected there."

"How do we prepare ourselves for the small deaths that happen so unexpectedly?" I asked Twin Dreamers.

"We gain the power because we cannot prepare for surprises life throws at us—loss, betrayal, disappointment, and on and on. Events can take you and fling you out of your reality. The struggle to recapture your balance is one of the mysterious gifts of life. These moments become gifts of strength, spiritual endurance, and power. To find your way back, you have to open your heart, not your mind, and let the healing of the Great Spirit flow through you. You will never be the same again."

In my way of seeing, there is no other way. There are many experiences, meditations, visualizations, so many ways to broaden your experience, but in the last analysis, to me, experience holds the secret. The experience of your own being is truly all that you have when you leave this earthwalk.

Time When the Trees Make Their Leaves

THE CACTUS AND THE RAIN

Asleep, I say to you,
let your dreams wake you up enough

for you to see
how the dreams can heal you.

Some truth in the unconscious
waiting to be understood

repeats itself in code,
cycles through your being

here to tell you
here to teach you

something you need
to know.

JACK CRIMMINS

ONE

Your Song

"You are walking in the footprints of the ancestors," Face in the Water said to me, her brilliant blue eyes reflecting the blaze from the central fire. We sat together in ceremony in the Sonoran Desert of Arizona.

"For many years I have listened to your words, your voice, in awe, Grandmother. You hold up a mirror for me that has been clouded by smoke as if your voice and your presence came from the world of spirit and not from this land."

Face in the Water looked down at the red chief's blanket we were sitting on. With her long, elegant fingers, she traced a thread of black wool woven in the pattern. I wondered at all her hands had touched in the many years of her life. She was so very old, and had helped so many with the goodness and wisdom of her soul. She lifted her hand, and as if touching a tiny bird that had fallen from its nest, she lay her fingers on mine and then settled her palm onto the back of my hand. Her generosity, the tenderness, the pleasure of her touch put me instantly at ease.

"You will fly away soon to do your work, little wolf. Your nest is being prepared."

"Will I see your face in my dreams, Grandmother? My confusion is deep. How do I teach my people about transition, change, and death?" I asked.

"In the Tree of Dreams there is a song," the old woman said. "Like any other living thing, it has a song to be sung. To lose your song is to lose your soul. The song in the trees is something to be listened for very, very carefully. It teaches you that life is never ending. This is what you can say to your people. So many of you in the Western world are looking at elderhood for the first time. Perhaps what I am going to say to you will help them."

Smoke from the fire whirled around us in purple-gray plumes, creating mysterious shadows in the air.

"As the leaves begin to drop from the tree in autumn," she continued, "an harmonic is created. The harmonic is different with every leaf that falls and different again for every tree. The Tree of Dreams is you and me. We are all a Tree of Dreams. We are filled with yearning, joy, and love. We are filled with the teachings that we have received and the experiences that we have had. Our branches are the different times of our lives. The leaves are the experiences—the colors, the textures, the aspects of the divine. As the leaves fall, the song can be heard, a new song that plays on the wind and is communicated to other trees, if they are listening.

"The whale people who live in the north speak about the great whale and how, when she sings a song, it is heard sometimes a thousand miles away. Another whale picks up that song, and the echo is heard another thousand miles away. This goes on until that song is created around the world by all whales singing in unison.

"The music that forms from the dropping of the leaves is similar. The song that was very much your own blends to create a harmony with other songs as it touches the earth. It is at that moment that all leaves become one, surrounding the earth with crimson, orange, red, and gold."

I watched this woman who was one of the oldest among us. She had never come out of the mists for me. She kept to herself, but she had touched my heart from the very beginning when Agnes Whistling Elk and Ruby Plenty Chiefs and I had paddled a canoe up river through the fog of the far north to the encampment of the Sisterhood of the Shields. I will never forget the luminous vision of forty-four shields painted and shimmering on their tripods, and each woman dressed in quills, bone, silver, turquoise, coral, beads, and ceremonial dresses, awaiting our arrival. The fire was roaring and the drumming began as we paddled silently around a turn in the slow-moving river and broke through the tule fog into the afternoon rays of sunlight. The women, old and beautiful beyond my imagining, stood and welcomed us. I had not known of their existence before that moment.

Face in the Water smiled as she watched my eyes. I could not look into hers for long. I looked this way and that and then I had to laugh before I could settle my eyes on hers.

"Do you feel better now?"

"Yes, thank you, Grandmother. There is so much I want to share, and I want to do it well. All of you have survived the hardships of reservation life so artfully. You have families, children, and professions, to say nothing of your sacred teachings! You have transformed the difficult times into strength and power. You have taught me to work with energy fields—if only I can do as well as you."

The old woman watched me, her eyes gleaming silver like frozen tundra around the glaciers in the north. For a moment I walked into her gaze and saw a glimpse of the ancient past, the tribal customs of her people. She carried all the beautiful memories of days gone by, just as we all do. But few have suffered losses as immense as those of native people. These elder women in the Sisterhood have survived difficulty with special practices. Their memories and history deepen them like an endless cave penetrating hundreds of miles into the center of the world—smoldering, molten earth and fire. This was her power, held deep within her. Face in the Water posessed great skill and knowledge, but she did not guard it jealously. She shared love and her knowledge freely to those who would listen.

"You have taught me the joys of elderhood. I want others to be inspired by that vision. I want to tell these stories well. I want to write a book, Grandmother, that has chapters in it that represent leaves falling from the Tree of Dreams."

"You have your song," she said. "You learned about the ways of power early in your work with us. As long as you have your song, you can never lose your direction or your vision. Remember, the owl will take you to your Tree of Dreams. You are not done here yet. The tree holds other dreamers who are waiting to help you. Don't stray off the track—you know that—follow your song line. It connects you to what is good and powerful for you. You live in both worlds. You live in spirit and you live on the earth. This is not an easy song to sing, but teaching the young ones to treasure their elderhood is the finest gift you can give, and you will do it well. As the leaves are falling, the new ones begin to grow. That is law. That is your story work. One of the joys of elderhood is telling your story. This is our power before we die. We can pass on what we've learned. Our legacy is thousands of years old. Let it flow through your lips. Anyone can take up a drum and talk to the Great Spirit and join you in a chant. It has always been that way. Your work here for the old ones is just beginning. I am here for you."

Suddenly, I was jolted back into the present reality by the wild honking of horns as our taxi came to an abrupt stop in front of my publisher's building in New York City.

"We're here, Lynn," Al said, reaching his hand out to help me from the back seat of the taxi. For a moment I stared at his hand, still seeing Face in the Water in my mind, the drums gently beating like a heartbeat in the distance of my reverie, now far away. Then it stopped. I bolted out of the taxi, wanting to be present and leave my dreaming behind. Al stared at me, wondering, and then took my arm in his as we strode through the spring sunlight and cool bursts of wind.

"You've only been back from visiting your teachers a few days—must have been hard for you—foot in two worlds and all." He laughed and guided me through the foyer and into the elevator.

Voices and clicking high heels echoed off the vast marble floors and vaulted ceilings of the building lobby. I turned and observed a sea of frantic eyes and tight smiles as the elevator door closed and divided us from those who were waiting.

Al nudged me. "You're musing again." I smiled at him, my friend and agent for so many years.

We had barely stepped through the glass doors of my publisher's office, when we were assaulted by a barrage of swear words coming from a furious young man with a red beard who was being thrown out of the building by two guards. I did a double-take—for a moment, I thought the man was Red Dog, an evil sorcerer I had known years before. But how could it be—Red Dog was dead, wasn't he? Now that I looked closer, I saw that this young man had dark hair and didn't resemble Red Dog at all. Yet a feeling of unease had taken hold in my heart just the same. Red Dog was my worst nightmare—a symbol of evil to me. I had seen him steal power from women. Many of us have a Red Dog in our lives, someone or something that is filled with darkness, but that also forces us to find our center and our strength. Red Dog had been my adversary, and our power struggle had brought me to my lowest point. Sometimes he had put me through what felt like small deaths for me, but I had grown despite him. Where had this vision come from? As suddenly as the vision of Red Dog had appeared, it was gone.

The man had been ushered out of the building, but his voice echoed down the hallways and book-filled cubicles. Shocked workers poked their heads up and out from everywhere around us.

"What in the world was that all about?" I asked a young woman who came to escort us to my editor's office.

"Who knows? Probably just another disgruntled author," she said, winking at me.

"Forget it," Al whispered, "just another nut case."

Right, I thought, taking a deep breath and following them down the hall.

TWO

Inside the Mystery

After our meeting, Al dropped me off at Tavern on the Green in Central Park to meet my girlfriend for lunch. I still felt uneasy from the vision of Red Dog. It was strangely real and it unsettled me.

"I want my life to be exciting," Jackie said.

She tossed her sleek auburn shoulder-length hair out of her eyes and sat staring at me, ready for a challenge. It had taken her years to get over her husband's untimely death, and I could see the pain etched into the lines around her eyes.

We were sitting on the patio under the trees. Birds were singing their spring songs. Sun filtered through the leaves and the arbor onto our table. A clean white linen tablecloth was spread beneath our plates. We were both eating omelettes and drinking coffee while talking about our lives, which seemed, at this moment, to be half over at least.

I looked out at the trees that were now tossing and blowing in a breeze that had come up from the south. The scent of grass and newly blooming flowers was carried on the wind.

"I want mystery in my life," Jackie continued.

"What does that mean to you?" I thought perhaps she was re-acting to her current problems with her second husband.

"I don't know. I guess I wouldn't be saying that if I knew," she responded.

"You know, sometimes I think that we look outside ourselves for answers. Look at my life when I first went to the Sisterhood of the Shields. When I found Agnes Whistling Elk, I was looking for the answer to the mysteries around me. I wanted excitement and meaning in my life, too. I simply could not live a regular or normal lifestyle. It wasn't for me; at least I thought so at the time. But I think, now, knowing what I know, I can do it. I know now that all of the excitement and the mystery, Jackie, is within us. Yes, I've been through extraordinary experiences. But if I was standing to-day at the top of La Caldera Canyon in the Yucatán jungle, I don't know if I could do what I did then. Walking that tiny precarious trail with a thousand-foot drop and then being stuck in quicksand by my teacher, Zoila, so that I could face my addictions . . . could I do that now? I don't know."

"But," Jackie interrupted, "what do you mean you couldn't do it? Of course you could! You say that you just want to live a peace-ful life. But you know what? There isn't anything about you that isn't yearning. All the years that I've known you, Lynn, you stretch every moment. Even during a walk to breakfast, you are looking for a piece of artwork in the windows that might broaden your horizons."

"All right, all right," I said. "I suppose I am rather restless."

"But it's important not to be an energy junkie or someone who lives on chaos. But right now, I want chaos!" Jackie laughed.

"I create flurries of energy," I said, interrupting Jackie's thought, "because I see that someone or a situation needs it to change or wake up. That's true. But I try to be very careful. Energy is powerful and you have to focus it in a certain way."

"I don't care whether energy circulates or if it's intended or not," Jackie said. "I just don't care. I want my life to be exciting, and I'm going to make it exciting. I'm going to leave my mean husband. I'm going to sell my house full of dreadful memories. I'm going to move from Connecticut and probably come out to where you are, to the Southwest—maybe to Arizona but probably to Los Angeles where my daughter is."

"Well," I said, "are you sure about this?"

"It's challenging," Jackie said, "because I don't know what the future holds. It's a choice, however, to break boundaries and to save my health. My husband is not a good man, and we've been very unhappy. He's so abusive, as you know."

"Changes are what most people cannot bear," I interjected. "That's the weakness I see in people. They hold onto the old patterns that work for them, that provide a living for them or a security, and they cling to them. There's nothing necessarily wrong with that."

"Well, I think there is. It's boring, and you get stuck. That was true for me for years, but I learned how to get free from confines. I admit I'm scared. But I have to do this or I'll die inside."

"I call the pain that you are suffering, Jackie, a small death. I think a series of small deaths prepares us to live fully and to die with a knowledge that there is truly life on the other side."

"How does that happen?" Jackie asked, now very pensive.

"Don't you find a new strength inside you? Don't you hear a voice shaping your decisions and urging you on?"

"Yes, I do. At first I thought it was an angel's voice, and then I realized it was my first husband. I'm closer to him now more than ever." Jackie put on her glasses and continued. "We've been friends a long time, Lynn. What are we going to find now? It's always scary to step into the unknown, but it is exciting!"

"A few days ago I went to see someone, Jackie. I want to tell you about her," I said. "Sophia was a person who lived her life on the edge of a precipice. She pushed the envelope of experience every day and gathered life to her with both hands. She was an artist in every sense of the word. Sometimes she behaved lovingly and sometimes not. But we all learned from her to expand and to enjoy. She had five husbands, several children, boyfriends. She ran a restaurant, worked as an artist and heaven knows what in between until she was about ninety. I can hear her now still, as I see the crows hopping on her beautiful adobe walls and smell the scent of piñon trees at her house. I can see the clouds above, throwing shadows over the pink walls.

"When I visited her, the house was filled with dogs, cats, people, phones, nurses, family, children—all guarding Sophia, and coaxing her to stay alive while her life force slowly slipped away. She passed the day after I saw her. I could see her spirit edging out of her body and going back into her. Surrounding her were guardian spirits of her family members who had passed on. They had come from the other side and were welcoming her. It was not a fearful passing. Instead, it seemed there was celebration in the air, not only from spirit, but also from those who loved her.

"It takes great strength to have the freedom to die with grace and allow the last of life to slip away gracefully. We all are faced with our own mortality, Jackie. You don't need to have constant excitement in your life to feel alive. But sometimes the small deaths—grief, loss, hard decisions—teach you how to live. Witnessing Sophia's passing, I could see that the amazing celebration of her life would continue on in the world of spirit."

We sat with our own thoughts for several minutes.

"I think you're making a good decision, Jackie," I finally said.

"I'm here for you always. I think you've made a bid for power—this is good. You know, I have a sense of danger right now, but it's coming out of the ether. I don't know what it is. I have a sense that something is about to happen in my life, too, and it's going to change it forever."

"Do you know something I don't?" Jackie asked.

"No," I said.

"Well great," Jackie laughed. "I know, excitement will happen to you, and I'll just be sitting here and reading your letters."

"Well, you could answer my letters." We both laughed.

Over the next few months I often talked to Jackie, but the next time I saw her, she looked reborn. She was bright and strong. She had left her abusive husband soon after our lunch, sold her house, and had moved near her daughter. She even had a new boyfriend.

"Wow!" I said. "Sometimes dreams come true!"

THREE

Spider Woman

That night in my hotel room, somewhere between sleep and consciousness, I had a premonition. I tried to go back to sleep, and the same images of Red Dog appeared again and again.

Ben and Drum, two of Red Dog's apprentices, were trying to jimmy the lock on Red Dog's cabin. Through the mist of my dreaming, I could see Ben and Drum, my old adversaries. We had played terrifying tricks on each other over the years. Now they were older, wiser, and yet still fumbling and foolish in their way. Suddenly, the door flew open with a crack and I nearly awoke. Even in my dream, I could smell the inside of Red Dog's cabin—stale, dusty, dark. What was happening? Ben and Drum searched for matches to light the kerosene lamp, but to no avail. Then Ben stumbled over something lying on the floor, and he smashed down, face first, yelling.

"What in . . . what . . ." Drum yelled in response.

They knelt down to find the body of their dangerous sorcerer and teacher, Red Dog. They looked at each other in disbelief, barely able to see each other in the gloom of the cabin. Drum leapt up, threw open the door, the windows, and the shades. Red Dog was still warm. If he was dead, he hadn't been dead for long. Ben and Drum had studied well their sorcery with Red Dog, and they knew exactly what to do. They felt for his pulse, but it was very faint, almost imperceptible. Perhaps he had suffered a stroke of some kind.

At once Ben and Drum began to do ceremony. They knew that Spider Woman was the only one who could save Red Dog. It was written. They were in search of the location of Spider Woman, for she held a sacred pouch. Even though Spider Woman was a member of the Sisterhood of the Shields, and their enemy, they knew of the ancient legend. She knew the song for life — the only song that would bring Red Dog back. They went into a trance and approached Spider Woman. They found her close by doing a sacred blessing for the life and death of a young child.

Ben and Drum were on their way. I could see them running through the darkness, getting into an old truck and driving down dirt roads, leaving huge dust clouds behind them, certainly not trying to be sneaky. Anybody within miles could have spotted them in the middle of this wilderness. The reservation is crisscrossed with dirt roads and washes, some nearly impassible to the average driver, but Ben and Drum were on a mission. They knew that they only had minutes to accomplish their task.

My dreaming suddenly took me to Spider Woman's consciousness. She was very aware that someone was after her, but she did not seem to be disturbed. In fact, she seemed to be welcoming them. I could hear her voice in my dream. She spoke to Ben and Drum, and she said, "You have come to steal from me — to steal something sacred. You have come, and it is written that the song should be given to you. But if it is not returned to me properly and with honor, then you will both be dead within forty-four hours."

That was all I heard. I knew something powerful was being transmitted to Ben and Drum. Spider Woman and her clan are mysterious and mostly unknown to people the world over, but she gave life to the people. This is the legend. She is the one who holds the secret of rebirth and death in the song of life. I have never heard that song; it is not part of my teaching, but I know that Spider Woman holds that secret. And I know that somehow Ben and Drum were given the memory of that song for only a very short time.

Suddenly, I could see the face of Spider Woman. I could hear her singing in the moonlight. Accompanied by a haunting melody, she was forming words that were strange to me. It was a short song and the words became discernable, one by one. I could see a language that I didn't recognize. Words as symbols swirled around me, and then they were gone.

Then the words followed on the wind. They reached Red Dog, still lying on the floor in his cabin. In my dream it appeared as though his life was definitely gone, but the words whirled around him. Ben and Drum were drumming and shaking a special rattle made out of hard leather. Powerful men they are—sorcerers, skilled in the ways of dark magic. I have witnessed their strength; I have a healthy respect and give them a wide berth as much as I can.

Red Dog came back to life from this song. I could see his spirit returning from far away, reentering his body through the top of his head. I saw life animating him. I witnessed this with great awe and with great trepidation as well. I had thought Red Dog was dead! I had been told this and I held it as truth for years and years.

Yet this was a dream. And so his return to life must also be part of my dream.

Suddenly I was awake. I was covered with perspiration. I leapt out of bed and stumbled into the shower without even turning on the lights. In the dark I stood under the warmth of the shower, still chilled to the bone. I shook my head, trying to banish the images from my mind. Slowly, the room became real to me again: marble, polished wood, soft white rugs, moonlight shining through the windows. The shower became real, and I touched my hands to the tile, trying to ground myself in the present.

What a strange dream, I thought. *Is this a sign of what is coming? Am I going to experience once again the presence of Red Dog? Oh, that cannot be,* I thought. If only I could pick up the phone and call Spider Woman. I sent out messages in the etheric fields, but nothing came. I remembered a turquoise doorway in the dream, leading into Spider Woman's adobe hut. I had stood before it, wanting desperately to open the door, but I was unable to move. I knew that there was a lesson here for me — something I knew to be true had been turned upside down. But what were these shadows about? Ben and Drum and Red Dog — what was their meaning in my life? They had already taught me so many painful lessons — how to fight for myself and what I believe to be true. Besides being evil, Red Dog was a symbol of how we grow. We grow by running into difficulties, pain, challenges. He challenges my balance and ability to choose healthy relationships and my fundamental passion for the light of the divine.

I couldn't go back to sleep, so I picked up the phone and called Jackie.

"Hi, are you sleeping?" I asked my friend.

"What do you mean, am I sleeping?" Jackie replied. "It's three in the damn morning."

"Well, I just thought I'd call," I said, listening to her fumble with her clock.

"That's nice, but do you think we could maybe have this conversation in the morning?"

"No, I need to talk to you. I'm frightened."

"What happened?" Jackie was suddenly alert.

"Well, you know what I've always said—that all the dreams that I've had in my life have been prophecy. Remember the dreams I had about Agnes Whistling Elk in the very beginning? Those dreams never gave me anything tangible. You know they don't give me dates. They don't give me specific cities or people. They just leave me with a feeling of shifting consciousness."

"You must have seen something in your dream," Jackie said, fully awake now.

"I didn't see anything exactly . . . Okay, I have to tell you the truth. I didn't want to scare you, and I didn't want to give it any reality, but I saw Red Dog lying dead on the floor, and then come back to life. Spider Woman, Ben, and Drum brought him back to life in my dream. I can't believe I'm saying this. What a dream! I'm sorry I woke you up. I'm just frightened. What are you doing right now? Could you come over?" I asked.

"Can I come over? Oh Lynn, I don't think so—not at this time!"

"All right. I'll talk to you in the morning."

"Yes, that would be a really good idea. Hey, Lynn, I'm glad you called. Don't ever hesitate."

"Thank you. Goodnight, Jackie."

Finally I fell into a fitful sleep.

In the morning, still exhausted, I drove to the airport and went standby on a flight to Canada. I had to see Agnes and Ruby. Something was amiss. I thought maybe it was my dream, but it had to be something more, for I felt inordinately unsettled. I could feel it in my solar plexus.

FOUR

A Piece Is Missing

"Agnes," I said, as the two of us walked across a meadow, poplar trees surrounding us. A hawk took flight from one of the higher branches, the morning light striking its harlequin feathers, making them glisten. "It's a wonderment to me—the trees are laughing. Their leaves are quaking, moving, exercising in celebration of their existence. At least it seems that way to me."

Agnes nodded and followed a deer trail, a narrow track through the meadow. Buttercups and corn flowers bloomed, shiny and fresh from the rain the night before. The smell of the earth was pungent.

"Look at the flowers," Agnes said. "They celebrate, too. Look at their beauty. Look at their excitement as the sunshine nourishes them. You can see it, you can feel it, can't you?"

She held the palm of her hand down just above the flowers. I did the same. I could feel the heat, gentle, sweet, tender. Agnes pointed toward the creek flowing green, copper, then silver, underneath the poplar trees. We set out across the meadow toward it.

As we walked, the breeze came up from the west, sending silver rivers through the grass. I took a deep breath of the fresh breeze, feeling my heart expand. Then apprehension came over me.

"Ah," Agnes said, "come, come sit by this water. Let's watch the creek for awhile."

We sat under old poplar and cottonwood trees, their bark gnarled and twisted, their branches touching in a canopy above us. The light filtered through the patterns of leaves, leaving reflection on the earth and the water flowing near us.

"I need to tell you my dream, Agnes. You're acting different somehow." I paused, but she said nothing. "I wanted to tell you my dream the moment I saw you, but I didn't feel that the time was right to approach you. I don't know why I hesitated, but I did. There's something in the air, I know it. Why is Red Dog in my dreams? I'm scared. Why is Spider Woman there?"

I went on to tell Agnes every aspect of my dream. She listened attentively with some surprise on her face.

"There are many premonitions in the air, black wolf," she said quietly, "maybe even in your dreams. There are changes coming and for the first time in your life, you are squarely facing the mirror of your own mortality. Red Dog and Spider Woman, too, are symbols of death and rebirth for you."

Agnes closed her eyes and gently rocked back and forth. She did this when she was accessing that place in the mystery where shamans go, a place of knowledge.

For a long time we said nothing. I felt better having spoken my dream out loud. As I watched the pink and copper colors of the sun reflecting off the current in the creek, I momentarily felt I was a part of the creek, flowing rivulets of water, affected by the air and the experience of all that was around us.

I mused about the book that I was writing. I realized that like life, my books seemed to have a vague beginning, middle, and end.

I have always written that way. Red Dog appears, turns me upside down, and then leaves. I want life to happen, to unfold. I don't want to put a structure to it and then try to make feelings and people and experiences fit into that structure. I've always written my books in a way that would allow the events to occur in a natural way, much like the flow of the creek. If the wind came up, there was more of a current. If it rained, the flow of the water would increase and then lessen, depending on the depth of the water.

We're like that, I thought. We move through life, using relationships as signposts, as markers. If our intimate relationships don't work out, then we move into the world, into a new social life, to find a new relationship in which we can, hopefully, build intimacy. We try and we fail, going back and forth, back and forth.

My apprenticeship with Agnes and Ruby and the Sisterhood has been completely without intention. I have never designed the patterns. I connect to the teachings from Agnes on something like a cellular level. I think women define life organically from their soul. I think if I had tried to define life in categories, I would have lost most of the teachings that I found.

My thoughts flashed again to Red Dog—to our great differences, and the many connections and bridges we had broken. Part of our reality was that we often lived a mythology unconsciously. For example, I am in the habit of attributing mysterious, mythical qualities to people, and often, without realizing it, I expect them to perform this way—like Lilith, constantly in pursuit of passion, or Persephone, who holds the keys to heaven and hell. Somewhere in my mind, I had turned Red Dog into a mythic figure who represented the shadows that my father had cast upon me, those parts of myself that were not healed. Symbolically, Red Dog was like Zeus, the mythic figure who impregnated the goddess Metis, or wisdom, and then swallowed her whole, so that her wisdom and creative power became his own. Then he gave birth to Metis's child, Athene, from his own head. Zeus, like Red Dog, wanted it all. Red Dog found the power of women by stealing it from them. He once said to me, "Your life is a mythology!" And of course, it was true.

Red Dog was an evil sorcerer who practiced magic and trickery. He had a strange appearance, sometimes ugly, but sometimes seductive and sexual. He was powerful because he could exhibit the characteristics of women and men. People like Red Dog act as they want to. Our interpretation of them might actually be quite different than the reality of who they are. I'm not saying that Red Dog wasn't evil, but deep inside me there was a resonance that made me react in fear. As a child I had always been wary of my dad. And it was hard now to live without that fear because it had become so familiar, almost like a friend.

We often unconsciously choose a disease that represents hurtful and negative feelings from childhood. Because we have always lived with these feelings and have never really healed them, we become ill. We justify ourselves through these feelings or relationships. I wondered now if I was somehow justifying myself in my struggle. Was I justifying my fear or trepidation about darkness or evil? I didn't want to believe the news in my dream that perhaps somewhere Red Dog was still alive.

"Someone may join us." Agnes interrupted the silence. "Someone that you have not seen for a long while."

I was immediately alert, dreading the thought of the person she was talking about.

"Who?" I asked timidly.

"Well," Agnes hesitated, building the suspense, "Spider Woman wanted to see you this afternoon. She came in my dreaming last night," Agnes said. "She wants to talk with you. She said she'd meet us down by the creek."

"Well, thanks for telling me," I said. "You know, she was in my dream, too."

"Yes, I know."

"Is anybody else going to appear?"

"No," Agnes said. "I think Spider Woman is quite enough for you to handle."

I had always been nervous around Spider Woman. She was a woman of immense power. She was the elder of the Spider Woman Clan. She held great secrets about life and death. It was fitting that I would see her now. She was a vision to see and experience. I took a deep breath and centered myself.

With a brief rustling of leaves, Spider Woman appeared downstream. She walked toward us, swinging her leather bag as if she were going to join us for a picnic. Agnes put her arms around Spider Woman. They hugged and signed to one another. We sat by the creek in the shade of a poplar tree and said nothing for awhile. We often visit this way, sitting in silence, feeling the energy and the love, allowing the quiet and the breeze to move gently through our hair and against our skin.

Spider Woman broke the silence with her eyes. She looked at me and I looked back. She wore a red kerchief around her head. Her grayish salt-and-pepper hair was pulled back in a traditional knot at the nape of her neck. She wore a long velvet skirt, black and full, and many strands of old silver, turquoise, and coral beads, so old that they seemed to have joined together. Her red velvet blouse was maroon and orange in the sun, and from her ears dangled silver earrings. In repose her countenance was extraordinarily fierce. Wisps of hair caught in the wrinkles in her skin. Her eyes, defiant and kind, watched every move that I made. Spider Woman was so beautiful. Why is it that we don't think that elder people with the magnificent lines of aging and time that etch their faces are attractive? The beauty and wisdom in the creases of her face were profound.

"Spider Woman, I have been having dreams about Red Dog. Dreams about you. Is that why you have come?" I asked.

"Yes, and I am here because there is something that you need to learn. You are facing your own mortality. That is disturbing for you. There are many places in our lives where we create a mythology about who we are. There are intimate relations that sometimes don't work, and when they fail, we go out into society and find new intimate relationships. We go back and forth in our lives, back and forth, wondering if we will ever find happiness. This is the essence of our existence, the beginning, middle, and end."

I nodded. Agnes sat with her eyes closed, listening out of respect.

Spider Woman took a herkimer crystal out of her medicine bag and held it up to the sun. It threw prisms of light across her face. She held it like a little bird and then handed it to me. Gently, I took it from her hand. It was warm. I held it to my heart and whispered "Thank you," to Spider Woman.

"Call me Pearl," Spider Woman said. "Everyone calls me Pearl."

I was very honored, and I nodded and smiled. Agnes laughed. I placed the crystal in a beaded leather medicine bag that I carried over my shoulder.

"You will need this crystal," Pearl said to me. I opened my eyes in question, but said nothing. "When you need clarity, take out that crystal. It is a mother crystal and it will give you light. I have used it and shared her beauty for many, many years."

"I am full, Grandmother," I said.

Pearl looked at me, observing me. Then suddenly, she stood up and skittered as if performing a dance step sideways. She was playing with the light between her hands, and doing something with her fingers.

Pearl looked at the sky and then at me and laughed. "You're afraid of me," she said.

"Well, no," I said. "Well, yes, I guess I am. It's the way you move," I finally said. I remembered her in ceremony so many times. I would feel something at my back as I stood up, and from across the circle she would somehow appear right behind me. I would turn around with a start, not understanding how she had moved there so quickly. She was an angular, thin woman, with tremendous agility.

She sat down again next to me. "We create dramas. We create the characters in our lives so often. Let's take Red Dog for an example. He has always been a symbol of evil for you. He represents challenge. He represents the darkness and the mystery. He was a dark soul. Let's think of your mythology. In ancient mythology, Inanna was the queen of heaven. She descended into the lower world to meet her sister, who was the queen of the underworld. Inanna was murdered, but she came back to life. She gave away her much-loved male partner to her sister, the queen of darkness, so that she could then emerge onto her own throne. During her absence, her man had taken her throne as his own. So giving him away to his death in the underworld seemed appropriate.

"Many of us experience something like mythology when we go into the shadow side of ourselves as we face death or illness or loss. Unexpected changes mean so much in our preparation for the understanding of our mortality. They deepen us so we can find the hidden meanings in our pain and our longing."

Pearl was very articulate. She placed her palms on the earth and said, "If you listen to mother earth, she will teach you everything." Then she raised her fingers to the sky. "Listen to spirit. The male spirit comes together with the female spirit of mother earth and they marry each other in the most beautiful of ways. This marriage is a dance within each of us.

"If you are afraid of things, don't look outside yourself, little wolf, look inside. Your fear of Red Dog—of his life, his death, or even his immortality—is a fear that you perhaps have not completely dealt with. Now it is time for you to understand. You learn well through experience, as we all do."

Again, Pearl lifted her fingers as if she were feeling the currents in the air or signing in a language unknown to me. Her movements had a subtle effect in my solar plexus. Then she settled her hands into her lap.

"I want to tell you everything," Pearl said, her eyes flashing silver in the light, "but I cannot take experience away from you and I cannot give it to you. So take your crystal, and use it to see me. I will dream you if that is your pleasure."

"Yes," I said hesitantly. "Pearl, I welcome your presence in my life."

"Take your crystal," she continued, "and hold it up to the sun. Hold it up to the moon. It will bring you clarity about the dreams. I will see you soon, little wolf. I will dance around you in the moonlight. I will be visible in the dawn, in the first rising of the sun. Listen to my voice on the wind, for I am here to teach you."

Pearl stood quickly, making a strange movement with her shoulders. She had a big smile on her face, her teeth white against her dark skin.

"I will see you in my dreams," she stated.

Agnes and Pearl threw their heads back and laughed. Then Pearl smiled at me and for a moment she held my hands. Then, skittering sideways, she walked quickly over to Agnes. She took Agnes's hand, and like two young girls, they walked together down the bank of the stream. I watched them with amazement as they rounded the bend in the creek and disappeared out of sight. They were like ghosts in the night, filling me at once with illumination and question, terror and beauty. And then I laughed. What an incredible dream, I thought, less frightened now. What an incredible experience! I thanked the Great Spirit for bringing these extraordinary women into my life for all these years. I took out the crystal and held it up to the sun so it reflected prisms of gold light.

There are emotional crystallizations, I thought, in our lives. Those are the things that drive us, that trick us into behaving in ways that do not serve us. I write from the inside of a woman's heart. We should always write about what we know. Relationships in our childhood have an impact on our lives and can make us break our connections with people. We destroy the bridges that might connect us to the innermost soul of someone. There is so often a place inside of us that needs healing that we can't seem to face. Those are the emotional crystallizations. Perhaps this was the case with Red Dog and me. I thought back to the terrible time when Red Dog captured the soul of my friend, July. He seduced her and tricked her; he took her innocence and power and trapped her soul in a gourd. Through our powers, Agnes, Ruby, and I wrestled her soul back. How often I have done soul retrievals with friends and put back together the fragmented parts of their being!

Symbolically or literally, we give away our power to people. We give away the power of our understanding. As we experience difficulty in our lives, we crystallize into something solid, rigid, unflowing, and we lose what we have come here to find. We have to understand it all, I thought, even things we don't want to speak of, such as sudden illness and the specter of mortality. These emotional crystallizations form the underlying core of what drives us from one experience to another if we are fearful. When we heal, we are transformed, and the next time we come from love.

Many people have said to me, "But I'm not afraid of death."

Then I watch them as they hide from themselves behind one addiction or another, not necessarily alcohol or drugs, but in relationships or codes of behavior. Have you ever seen people who hide behind a rigid sense of respectability? And then they sink into patterns of behavior that render them senseless, at least in regard to what they need to learn in this life. We are here to evolve into a higher consciousness. To do that, we must run up against barriers over and over again.

Red Dog is one such barrier for me. When I thought of him, I went into a place inside myself that was cold and unfeeling and tinged with blackness, the color of shadows at twilight. I needed to learn how to bring light into those shadows—but I needed help.

I rose from my sitting position as Agnes came back around a curve in the creek. She was smiling and walking rather swiftly. She came toward me, rubbing her tummy, and said, "Come, let's go eat. I'm hungry." And off we walked toward the cabin together.

Late that night in my dreams I saw luminous fibers waving in the sky on the wind. They were very tiny, thin fibers, like a spider web. A great red-colored elk came into my vision and touched the fibers with her nose and disappeared. Then I flew up into the sky and traced my fingers along them. I heard a voice in my head saying, "Follow, follow along." I followed the web until I came to another luminous thread, extending in another direction, perpendicular to the first. I felt it with my fingers as it waved gently in the currents of air.

The sky was very dark. I saw the Pleiades above me. Billions of stars shone blue like tiny holes in the fabric of darkness that surrounded me. I was not afraid. Somehow in my dreaming I felt protected. I could feel an energy like a silken cocoon surrounding and protecting me. I traced the threads and traveled along at the speed of light. It was vast, this web. I could see it out in front of me now. It went off onto the horizon of darkness, silvery, reflecting the light of the moon, but I didn't go beyond our constellations, our universe. The web seemed to turn and move around the earth so many hundreds of miles beneath me. I could see the continents and a magnificent view of the earth—the globe that is my world. There was something peaceful about being out in space like this looking down at my home. It filled me with happiness and joy, and I found myself laughing in the dream. Laughing and wanting to go further and further.

Then I heard the voice of Spider Woman. "Go back now, black wolf," she said. "Go back."

I turned around like a beacon of light moving from shadow to shadow, and I swept down through different aspects of the web.

"It's beautiful, isn't it?" Spider Woman asked.

"Yes, oh it is so vast," I said, still traveling quickly toward earth. I noticed now that the web was all around the world. "It's all around the earth," I said to Spider Woman.

"Yes," she replied. "We've woven the World Wide Web," she laughed.

That was the last I heard. I awakened from this dream and sat upright in bed. The dream had excited me. Sometimes it's difficult to go out of your body, but I knew that I could do it. I knew now that I could follow the mysterious teachings of Spider Woman. That was something to be thrilled about. I lay back down and fell into a deep, dreamless sleep.

FIVE

Move with the River

"Come, let's walk over here by the creek," Agnes said. "Come, black wolf."

I walked over to the creek with her, moving along in my bare feet. Both of us had removed our shoes and socks, and I felt the sand oozing up between my toes, cool and soothing. We sat finally with our feet in the creek water, cold and clear this time of year.

"Agnes, I dreamed with Spider Woman last night," I said, excited.

"Hmm." Agnes smiled. "Did you see her web in the sky?"

"Yes! I even traveled along it—so magical!"

I could see she was pleased for me. "I have always been your teacher," Agnes said, walking a short distance from me. "When first I heard your voice, the world changed for me, too. You could not know it, but I wept that first night with happiness. I could finally entrust the sacred songs to you. All was held together by your voice. The singing of the songs of life were to be put together with your words, your writing. Because of that, you were the very spirit of my dreams."

"Agnes." I placed the palm of my hand over my heart. Never had she spoken like this to me. I could say nothing.

"When the dusk comes, there will be more dreaming. Allow Pearl to speak to you. She may come to you as a small bird. She calls it Meena. She will fly into the canyons of your furthest imaginings. There is life on our great mother earth, and there is death. There is also an earth wind that shakes the trees to and fro. The Tree of Dreams sways, too. There is a great white cloud that comes from the rainy mountains. When it floats above you and rains upon you, the old songs of immortality will be sung to you."

Agnes sat down on a flat rock next to me and smiled into my eyes. Then, clearing her throat, she went on. "You see, you feel a sense of discipline," she said.

"I do," I answered.

"Discipline is misunderstood in your world. Even by you. Even with all that we have done together. Discipline is a process. It's not an end. Somehow, I think, black wolf, that your training early on in your life was about controlling yourself. You were in a Catholic school. You were trying to discipline your mind and your habits and your practice. But don't you see that this practice they taught you did not belong to you? Symbolically speaking, you cannot always take a costume or a tradition that is created by someone else for their ceremonies and expect to put that costume or ritual on and experience the same sacredness that they had. That's because it's not your costume. You need to design your own."

"Are you saying that I need more discipline when I'm dreaming, Agnes?" I asked, taking a pebble and tossing it into the water.

"I'm saying that discipline isn't an act of control. Discipline is an awareness. It's something you come to. It's like purpose — purpose you discover in your life. Purpose is not something that you make happen. You cannot invent passion, but you can uncover it. I think societies today have taken over someone else's ceremonial clothes. In other words, they learn from borrowed knowledge, not necessarily their own experience. They are wearing someone else's costume. It has been told to them that it is theirs, but it is not. It doesn't fit them. The energy of it is dead for them. There is no power in trying to control yourself in a way that someone else did. It may have worked for them, but it won't work for you."

"But Agnes," I said after thinking for awhile, "I am listening to your words. That's true. I am not trying to control myself in the way that you do or Ruby or Pearl does."

"That's right. We have never asked you to do that. We just ask you to define your own sacred life. Ruby and you and I are vastly different. And your discipline will be different. It's hard for you, isn't it, when you leave us and you go back into your world? You find it hard to move into the discipline of society, because it's not what we have together. We are very free-flowing," she said.

It was getting a little darker outside. The shadows were slanting through the trees and elongating in the forest around us. It was as if a whole community of shadow beings had joined us and circled us. As the wind came up, they began to dance. It brought a smile to my face. I loved being there with Agnes.

I laughed with her. "How true," I said. "It's true."

"Yes, and you have many wolf cousins that feel the same way. The original teachers, the wolves, teach each other. You like to teach, and you like to learn. You would never retire. You would never stop, because it is what you are. But when you feel like a dam in the river, it's not so good. You want to let the river flow."

"Isn't that what happens," I said, "in relationships? We dam up our energy, don't we? We try to hold onto something. We try and keep it the first way we ever experienced it. We want it to stay that way, because it's such a miracle to feel that love as it flows for the first time."

"Yes," she said, "it's true. It's another act of discipline that is in-correct—it becomes the need to control too tightly. Just remember, when you are accomplishing something in this life, it's like walking across the creek."

She was pulling me, now, across the creek. I held my skirt up to my knees, as did she. We stood in the middle, and the water flowed around us.

"You see, this is what people do. They stand in the middle of the creek, and then they don't move. They don't move with the flow. They stand and try to hold onto something, never moving. So the water, the flow of energy, has to move around them. Move with the water," she said, holding my hand, taking me downstream slowly, the rocks underneath our feet slipping and sliding.

"Ooh, soapstone," I said, kneeling down and picking up a peb-ble, slippery to the touch and brown. "Gosh, we used to have a lot of this when I was a kid, outside of Spokane, Washington. What we call soapstone."

As we walked a little farther, the creek became stronger.

Agnes said, "It's stronger, don't you see? It's moving down a bit, and the current is increasing. This happens in life when we get scared. We want to control the current to suit our needs—make it comfortable for us. It's all about control. When you try to control and repress your feelings, your intuitions, your character to please someone else, it is a lie," she said.

"Yes," I said. "I have seen it over and over again with all my people. We all repress aspects of ourselves so we can fit in."

"That's your sadness. The entire human race is sad, and it's because you are repressing and controlling all sorts of thoughts and feelings. Again, you are trying to wear someone else's sacred costume. Don't do it," she said. "You are not Indian."

We laughed and nodded in agreement.

"But I am," Agnes said, putting her fist over her heart. "I am an Indian woman. But I do not ask you to be Indian. I ask you to listen to the truth that we have memorized. I give it to you with open hands and an open heart. It is for you to decide how to teach this, how to bring it to others, and how to incorporate this truth into your own life. It is a process, always a process. As this creek flows where we're walking now with the current, it flows and we follow it. You follow the knowledge. It's not a stasis, is it?"

"No," I said, "you're right."

I tripped, and Agnes caught me by the elbow. We walked off to the side of the creek where we had left our shoes a long time earlier. I dried off my cold feet with the hem of my skirt and brushed off the sand.

Agnes and I looked at each other, exchanging a tremendous understanding of the universe and the world around us. We were not the same. We would never be the same. But we are of one spirit, one light, and I felt it to the core of my being.

SIX

Pulling Down the Clouds

Agnes, Ruby, and I sat in rickety rocking chairs on Ruby's porch, sipping sage tea together. I wanted to talk.

"Ruby, how do you explain transfiguration, the complete meltdown of what you thought was true in life? For instance, I thought Red Dog was dead and now he may not be," I said.

"Don't ask me questions. I'm like a girl working in the general store. I can't do two things at once," Ruby said. She grinned to herself, shaking her head, swishing her long braids back and forth over her red flannel shirt.

"What?" I asked.

"'What?'" she mimicked, her gray-blue eyes flashing momentarily, like a timber wolf sensing a rabbit.

"How did I get here? I need to understand my beginnings. What brought me here in the first place? I lifted my empty places up to you and Agnes. I asked you to help me understand the world that I . . ." I searched for words.

"Woman carries the sacred void," Agnes said simply.

"Yes, but my . . ."

"Your empty places held all possibilities because they contained nothing—another reason you were able to learn and develop your *Seeing*. You were innocent and there was nothing in the way."

"You mean, I had no beliefs?"

"Do you remember that time long ago when we went riding," she asked, "and we let the horses graze in a meadow, and we sat with a pile of stones—I call them the stone people?"

"Yes, and you asked me to put a stone in the center of the circle to represent each of my beliefs."

"That's right, little wolf. You built a huge pile of stones representing your beliefs—honesty, kindness, courage, all that stuff."

She smiled as I frowned.

"Agnes, it took me a long time to live through those stones, but I eventually realized that our beliefs can form a fence around our consciousness. I realized that you could be honest without believing in honesty so rigidly. You taught me that you can't learn beyond your set ideas. If I said to myself, 'I'm going to jog to the pier and back along the beach,' that's probably exactly how far I'd get. But if I simply jogged, I could probably go farther."

"Come, Lynn, let's take a walk," Agnes said.

"Well!" Ruby said indignantly. "Thanks for leaving me behind."

I grabbed my walking stick and followed Agnes as Ruby stomped into her cabin in a make-believe huff.

Agnes and I sat in the center of one of our ceremonial grounds, surrounded by huge craggy rocks and boulders. We were drawing symbols in the earth with a couple of sticks.

"Maybe I'm not the person you think I am," Agnes said to

me, looking at the cross of the four directions that she had just drawn.

"What do you mean?" I asked.

"Maybe I'm not who you think I am," she repeated.

"I'm not sure who I think you are anyway," I said.

"Well, who do you think I am?" Agnes said.

"I think you're a shaman of great power and magic and beauty."

"Thank you," Agnes said, swiveling her head around to look at me, like an owl in the middle of the night.

"Agnes, what are you saying? Is that not true?"

"Could be," she said with a smiling undertone.

I sat in silence for awhile watching her and then started drawing more designs in the dirt, smoothing them over with my hand and starting over again.

Agnes drew a circle and said, "What does this mean to you?"

"It means life, that we are a circle, that our lives are a circle and with each first step we take, we take our last step at the same time."

"Whuu! How philosophical of you!" Agnes said, laughing.

"That's what it means to me," I said.

"What if I told you that this was actually a square?"

She erased the circle and drew a square.

"I'd say, well, that's a square, and before, you drew a circle."

"That's true, but what if I told you from the very beginning of your life that a square was a circle?"

"Then I guess I'd think that a square was a circle."

"See?"

"See what?" I asked. "I don't know what you're getting at."

She waited a long time to answer me. I watched the wind blow a little dust devil down the sandy draw, raising sand and pieces of dried leaves in a circle into the air.

"What I'm saying," Agnes said, "is that what you see is not necessarily what you think you see. And who you are is not necessarily who you think you are. To understand that there is a world of spirit living right alongside of us, that there is so much more to life than what we see, is to prepare yourself for the curve balls that life throws us."

I let out a big sigh. "I understand you, but are you also trying to confuse me?"

"Could be," she said, "but not this time. What I'm really trying to do is to make you think with your body-mind, not with your brain. I'm trying to make you perceive from that place of power around your navel." She placed her hand on my midsection. "Now, you see me in a certain way, and I see you in a certain way. That does not mean that it's true. It's part of the illusion, the dream of this physical dimension. It is our life, and we make an agreement to see this dream or life in a way that seems to be appropriate for all of us.

"If you think you see somebody in a certain way, then you expect them to act in a certain way. That's part of the illusion, and that's part of what makes you confused and eventually sad. What if I didn't act like a shaman? What if I was wearing a little cotton dress, pushing a cart in a grocery store, buying cupcakes for my bridge party with all my little old lady friends, our hair tied up in curlers on our heads?"

"Bridge!" I exclaimed. "That's what my mother used to play."

"Exactly."

I sat and thought about that for a while, laughing to myself as I looked at my magnificent teacher, her grey braids glistening in the sunlight. The antique shield hanging around her neck was old and lovely. Her face was creased by time and humor. Her eyes glittered like fine crystal. Everything about her demeanor held an aura of power and charisma, but she was not always that way. Sometimes

she appeared as a completely different person—it was
affect me.

"What if I was wearing support stockings and a blue dress with
cornflowers on it and carrying a big old leather purse and all I
talked about was my aches and pains? And I limped and struggled
behind the grocery cart with no aura or charisma? Would you still
think I was a shaman?" Agnes asked again. "Don't you expect your
boyfriend to act in a certain way? Your friends, your publisher?
Your daughter? It's all part of illusion. That's what I call getting
caught in the dream. That's all a lie. You also cannot be the apprentice, the writer, the healer, the woman I expect you to be. And
that is good. You are black wolf."

I scratched my head, wondering where she was going with all of
this.

"What I'm trying to get you to do is loosen up," she said. She
shook my arm, getting me to relax my shoulders. "I want you to see
that if you believe that something is a square when actually it's a
circle, then you will probably believe that for all your life. Lynn, I
am trying to prepare you for what lies ahead. You feel unsettled because there are some changes in the wind."

"What . . . what are you talking about?" I said, suddenly appre-
hensive and yet enjoying the sense of adventure.

"I don't know that," she said, "but life is full of change. It is law.
It has always been that way. The *what* is for you to discover."

Agnes stood up and walked toward the hill. I followed her.
The wind had died down and the wilderness was silent except for
three ravens atop a juniper tree. Great white clouds were gathering
above us.

"You must imitate the exact event you desire," she said as she
knelt down and touched the rain-soaked earth from the night before. "Like this ground that has drunk its fill, you must saturate

your being with whatever it is you are looking for. Follow your ideas about death, life, and immortality. Understand that you are pulling down the clouds." Agnes pointed to the sky. "You are calling for rain in your heart so that your spirit can grow."

There was soft thunder from the north as we headed back.

"We will sing tonight," Agnes said as we gathered brush for the evening fire.

SEVEN

The Moon of Rain

When I awoke in the morning in Agnes's cabin, Agnes and Ruby were already dressed, drinking their coffee. I rolled out of my sleeping bag, sat down in a chair at the table, looked at them, and smiled happily. Ruby snickered. The trees were blowing in the wind. A thunderstorm was threatening.

"I am feeling great," I said to Ruby.

"Happy?" she said, laughing. "That's good news, black wolf." Ruby got up to pour a warm addition to her coffee. She slurped on the edge of her cup and set it down. Then she turned around and did a little jig and stood with her hands on her hips, looking at me. She picked up her coffee cup and loudly slurped some more.

"Space," Ruby finally stated. They often began a lesson this way—challenging me to explain the deepest meaning of a word.

"Yes," I answered, surprised. "I can't think. But I have a few words. I feel the space inside my heart like the desert, where distance is my god."

Ruby sat down, nodding her head. The women didn't say anything for quite some time. I was still, feeling calm and completely grateful for all that they had given me.

Agnes, reading my thoughts, commented, "You know, Lynn, you are ready."

"Ready for what?" I asked.

"For a new mountain to climb," she said with a wave of her hand. "You are preparing for something that you have never really taken on."

"What is that?" I asked quietly. A slow apprehension was beginning to build in my heart.

"You are approaching the moon of rain. It rains a great deal, but then the rain ceases to fall and the desert returns and the cactuses bloom, displaying their spring beauty," Agnes said. "Sometimes the clouds don't come and the rain is late and the corn and the grass do not grow. Then your thirst will transform your spirit."

"And you will drink the nectar of the thunder beings," Ruby stated very clearly.

"There are many threads to be woven together," Agnes added, observing my reaction.

I thought about their words and how they expressed the simplest nature of life: rain, corn, earth. "Where do I fit in?" I finally asked.

"You summon the clouds," Agnes said. "You must allow the many things that will happen to you. You must accept them completely, just as the earth and the cactus fill up with rain. You take your spirit back. Not only for yourself, but for us."

"What are you saying to me?"

Ruby poured a cup of coffee and brought it to me.

"You see, you have taken your spirit back. Once you gave us so much power in your life that it took a long time for you to become the mentor and the teacher you have become. You had so many things that you had to learn from us. So it was understandable. This has not been an easy path for you, but you dreamed your song years ago, and it is a magic song. Your song calls upon the powers of nature, and they are coming."

"Is that what you mean by 'rain'?" I asked.

"Of course," Ruby said. "It's the rain that helps the seeds to grow."

"Agnes, we have been working together for years, and I know that I have learned many things, but at this moment I want to know clearly what you mean. Who is coming? I feel like you have opened up the world of spirit for me and—"

"No." Agnes stopped me, holding her palms toward me. "Stop right there. We can't open up spirit for you. Only you can do that for yourself."

Ruby and Agnes stood up and started to wash a few dishes. For some reason they wouldn't speak to me. At times like this I leave them alone. They opened a window even though a thunderstorm was gathering and the wind was blustering. There was a crow, big, black, and shiny, sitting on the windowsill. He seemed to follow us wherever we went, looking for a handout, which he usually received. If he didn't get what he wanted, he would make a terrible ruckus, cawing and cawing and bobbing up and down.

I put on my clothes and opened another small window under the tin Coca-Cola sign that was nailed onto the wall to cover up leaks of air and rain in the old boards at the corner of the cabin. Then I got a match and lit a little candle that I had brought. I stared at the light of the flame for a while, sorting through my feelings. I thought of the rain and thunder and the wind-swept clouds that I love. I kept wondering what was coming.

"You have a way of seeing and feeling magic," Agnes said. "But to feel that magic, you have to be whole, and your spirit has to live inside you. It cannot be lent out in little pieces to anyone else. You can share your love, but you cannot share your spirit. We will explain about the rain, but not until we do ceremony tonight. The pain in your heart needs to be healed. So fast now and prepare yourself. We will talk later."

"My heart ceremony?" I asked.

"Yes," Ruby stated flatly.

Agnes sat down at the table, taking bunches of grass and branches and herbs that she had collected earlier. She was now tying them into bundles to be hung from the rafters in her cabin. Her face was impenetrable.

"I'm going out for a walk," Ruby said. "I think I am going to go out and look at the birds and stand in the rain."

The next morning I followed Agnes down a path toward Ruby's cabin, feeling strong and healed from the ceremony the night before. Dwarf pine trees lined our way. Several of the branches at the top were dead, and crows and hawks circled in the sky above us before landing on the gnarled gray branches.

"I have always felt during my years of apprenticeship with you that you held something inside—something that you kept secret and were trying to protect against invasion, from my complete understanding."

I looked up at the morning sun and the tree tops throwing filigree patterning on silvery leaves. They offered a gateway to the sky, but inside myself I felt something holding back. I couldn't step forward into the light.

"So often that's the way I've felt, Agnes. In my yearning to understand the spirit, I have discredited the physical in some way, as if my blood and my body were not respectable enough to be heard. Yet in my experiences and wanderings with you, I think I have bridged that gap at long last. I have spent times with you that are beyond description, years of discovering the sacraments of choice. And I am discovering that in my heart there has been a hidden landscape. Slowly but surely, I see that as we are spiritually, so we become physically. For example, if I'm afraid of success, I back away from it and my back begins to hurt."

"I do have a secret," Agnes said, placing her hand over her heart. The turquoise green of her bracelet of looped beads matched the colors in the shallow part of the creek water. "My secret is hidden in the lightning and the thunder. It has a color, but it is the color of our remembering—our remembering from a far history," Agnes said, looking toward the horizon. "We have created landscapes together in our work, and we have seen mountains and rivers and events that have imprinted our souls and burned our eyes. What we choose to ignore in life changes us and makes us prisoners of what we refuse to see. But do not despair, because we are moving into a time of new form. We are, piece by piece, through disintegration and the friction of heat and creativity, living in a great time of change. Maybe we won't learn the secret on a conscious level, but we are still becoming that secret.

"At one point our destiny becomes clear. I think that our lives are like that. The secret is being born within you. There is a kind of truth ahead of you, black wolf, a truth that you have not seen before."

"How do I find it?" I asked. "Please, Agnes, talk to me. I can't stand the suspense."

"It is something to be discovered. And you will. You have a life that is well examined and you often ask questions that are unanswerable. But you are going to find the scent. And then, as abruptly as the wind changes, you will see the changes that will affect you forever. Those changes have to do with your depth of love, including all that you have thought was your destiny. And then the disturbance you feel now will lift, as if taken by spirits in the night. In the morning glow, you will not be so heavy anymore.

"Come," Agnes said. "Come sit by me on this grass by the creek. I want to tell you something before we leave." Agnes took my hand as we began to walk.

"How many loves does it take to find the one love that is bound for you? The love that is golden and yet seems forever hidden from you?" Agnes asked, not wanting me to answer. "There is devotion, and there is your incredible ability to share affection. Hanging, like an echo in the wind, it is your love that blows hither and yon. It circles the beloved in a sacred dance that perhaps is never ending. But for you this dance holds the secret. Soon you will discover that secret. You have seen it in me, and now you see it again, held in another way inside yourself.

"Early in your life it was held by the stones and the rocks and the waters of the earth. And that is still true. Remember the flowers in your backyard that jumbled around in the lilac bushes? But nothing throbs like the aura of love that surrounds you now. Come to it. Be separate from it. And then, after your departure and your questioning and your doubt, become whole with it, for it is your future."

While she was talking, Agnes had been gathering a fistful of beautiful flowers that bloomed around us. She handed them to me and bowed her head gently, saying, "Here, for your new heart. For your new place of wholeness and worship."

A bouquet of flowers says it all, and I accepted her nourishment, the grace of her words. I surrounded myself with the cloak of wonderment and brightness that Agnes is to me and that life is to me. I thanked the Great Spirit for bringing me back to a place of curiosity and innocence. Until our ceremony, I hadn't ever realized my broken heart. That's how much I had hidden from myself.

"Your path in life up to this point, Lynn, has been to always be quite public with your feelings and who you are. You could say that it's as if somebody had turned your pockets inside out. Be careful that that does not become your shape. Nothing is wrong in people knowing who you are and in talking about following your dreams so that other people will have the courage to do the same. But all that is exquisite in life is inner. It is inside you, and that means that it is also very private to you and to you alone. So the deepest part of our relationship is very still. It grows in the darkness, in a sense. It remains very close inside both of us. It's like seeds planted in the earth—for they need darkness and a deep bed. A very intimate quality remains deep in your own heart and in mine. There is a privacy that is never communicated in words. It is communicated through the heart, and it can never be taken away."

EIGHT

Drawing the Bowstring

"We're going south," Ruby said, slamming in through the kitchen screen door. "A storm is coming. It's cold. We're going south."

"It's very hot in the south," I said.

"I don't care. We're going south to New Mexico when you go home to Los Angeles."

"You love cold."

"No, someone is coming."

"What do you mean, someone is coming?" My back crawled with anxiety.

"You are about to move into an experience that I hope you're ready for," she said.

"What do you mean?" I repeated.

"Someone is coming," Agnes said. "Someone's coming for you."

"What? The Four Horsemen of the Apocalypse?"

"Well, you could call it that."

I was now getting very nervous. They never said anything like that to me lightly. It meant something, and I knew it.

"Oh, yes, we mean something. Here, doggie, doggie, doggie," Ruby called from the porch outside.

Thunder rolled along the ground. Sizzling shafts of lightning split the sky. Rain came down intermittently, and the wind was blowing. It was powerful weather. I suddenly felt really scared, but a thrill of excitement also ran through me.

"Ruby, what do you mean, 'doggie, doggie, doggie'?"

"It's like 'kitty, kitty, kitty,'" Agnes said.

I watched them playing.

"Oh, no. Don't tell me you're calling for Red Dog?"

"It's possible. How are your dreams?"

"My dreams are strange, I must say."

"You see, power is already playing with you," Agnes said, reaching her hand out to mine.

"I think you are about to see what we've been talking about. You will learn a very great lesson, so maybe you're incubating," Ruby said. "Maybe you're just sitting on your eggs, and you just have to keep them warm until they decide to hatch. Maybe you're not giving birth at all. Maybe you're hatching eggs."

"Oh, for heaven's sake," I said. "What difference does it make?"

"It makes a lot of difference," Agnes said. "Because if you're incubating, which I think you are, then you are drawing the bowstring and getting ready to shoot your arrow. It's not ready yet. Polish your bow."

"Ah," I groaned. "Is there something happening that involves Red Dog?"

"Perhaps, considering what your dreams have been. You saw him in your dreams, Lynn."

"Yes, I did. The dreams were frightening and scary and red."

"Hmm, that's quite a coincidence, isn't it?" Ruby said.

"Why do you keep calling 'doggie'? That's really aggravating." I picked up a moccasin I had been working on for a few days and threaded the needle.

"Oh, I thought that maybe Red Dog's spirit was out here in the trees," Ruby said. "Maybe he would come visit for a while. Have some sage tea."

"Thanks," I snapped as I jabbed the needle into the moccasin and punctured my finger. "Ow!" I bled onto the moccasin and the table. I leapt up to find a rag to wrap around it. Agnes put a little bit of her special salve on it, then took some red material, soft and old, and wrapped my finger.

Agnes said, "See? It's time. It's the time of blood. A time of reckoning for you, my little black wolf. You see, it is never ending. The lessons never stop. You are just at the beginning, perhaps at the beginning of this circle where you began many long years ago. You're seeing it as if for the very first time."

Time When the
Leaves Turn
Dark Green

Who can give us
the breath of memory?

Without the dream
I have no voice

and She Who Walks with the Wind
did not die.

There is a time
for something else besides this death

we've all agreed to.
The cactus and the rain

teach us about
the old women and men who carry

the vibrancy of the young
with knowledge.

This new singing
is the chant of earth.
In the desert, the silence speaks.

NINE

Pink Flamingo

We were having lunch in the garden of the elegant Bel Air Hotel in Los Angeles. Once an old stable, it had been transformed by lavish gardens, gorgeous rooms, and haute cuisine. I was seated with two of my closest friends from college, Pat and Bev. A fountain glistened and trickled gently in the background. The high eucalyptus trees rustled and sang a gentle song in the light ocean breeze coming up out of the west. It was wonderful to see my girlfriends. We had known each other for more than twenty years. We had gone different ways in our lives. Pat was divorced with kids, an attorney, and she lived in New York City. I became a writer and had very different experiences than I thought I was going to have earlier in my life. Pat, however, had always wanted to be a lawyer and had been a very good trial lawyer all of her adult life.

"Are you happy?" Bev asked, her blond hair shining in the sun. She was always sleek, well groomed, and vivacious. She was also a mother and worked as an elementary school teacher.

As I thought about the paths we had taken and the choices we had made, I blurted out, "Life is so different from what we thought it would be."

"Yes," she said, "I can say that I truly am. However, there are moments when I think of us baby boomers facing old age—death—and I can't believe it."

"Me, either. It's around the corner, and I feel that I've wasted most of my life living for my family," Bev said. "I'm leaving education. And I'm going to finally act on my art degree and paint again."

"An atelier in Paris?" I asked. "That's great, Bev, really! Just kidding."

"No, a studio in Santa Fe."

"What about your husband?" I asked.

"He'll be there studying archeology. We are still good together, thank God!"

"Well, sometimes I'm terrified," Pat interrupted, looking sad. "I feel so out of control. Time is flying by, and I can't stop it." We nodded and sipped our drinks.

I had been married in this hotel years ago, I mused to myself, as hotel personnel bustled and flustered over wedding decorations around the swan pond below us. They were trying to arrange two pink plastic flamingos with white bows around their necks.

"Pat, how are you doing with Bill?"

Bill was her current significant other. Tears welled up in her eyes. She tossed a crumb to a sparrow hopping on the edge of our table.

"Bill left me the day that my mother died," she said, tears streaming down her cheeks.

"The day that your mother died?" I asked in disbelief.

"He called me in the hospital in Pittsburgh where I was sitting by her bedside with the rest of the family. He said that after our two-year relationship that he didn't think this was for him and that he was going to Europe with friends and that we were through."

Bev and I sat there, our mouths hanging open in shock, disbelief written all over us.

"How could someone do that?" Bev finally said.

"I don't know," Pat answered. "I asked if I could come see him, if we could meet somewhere and talk about it, if there was something I had done."

That registered in the back of my mind because Pat always thinks that somehow, no matter what, it is her fault, when in actuality she tries harder and loves more than almost anybody I've known.

"He wouldn't meet me," Pat said, "and that was it. Basically, that was the end."

"Did you know this was coming? Had anything started to happen? Was there another woman?" Bev asked.

Pat said, very carefully and quietly, that he had managed to lose a lot of money on drugs. He seemed to like to live on the edge. For him, that meant being high, being slightly scared, on the edge of losing all of his money at all times.

"But he's a conservative businessman," I said. "That just doesn't seem to fit."

"He was a great businessman," Pat said. "He made a lot of money in investments. But he was drawn to the high, the confusion, and the instability of the stock market."

We sat in silence. I reached out to Pat and held her hand. Out of the corner of my eye I saw one of the pink flamingos splash into the pond and a nervous young woman wading in after it.

"So Pat, what now?"

Several minutes went by as she gathered herself together. Then she looked at both of us with a big smile. "You know, I've spent my whole life being ill."

"Being ill?" I asked. I had always seen darkness around her heart, but she had never been willing to speak about it until now.

"I never thought that I was pretty enough or smart enough to have a whole, healthy relationship," she said.

"But how can that be, Pat? You're one of the most beautiful women I've ever known."

Bev and I looked across the table at this statuesque woman, tanned, wearing gorgeous jewelry and clothes, with a stunning figure and big soulful eyes. How could this be? She had hidden it all so well.

"I was never good enough. Do you know what I mean?" Pat said. "Even when I was in high school I got straight A's. But they were never good enough grades. If I got an A, my parents wanted to know why I didn't get an A-plus. If I was good in sports, they wanted to know why I wasn't better. Basically, I could never win. I never did well enough for anyone to be happy with me. So I rebelled and started playing hooky from school. I got involved with drugs, and I got involved in sex."

"Sex!" we both said.

"Yes, I got involved in my passion. I have just been discovering what that means to me. It doesn't mean what it means to most people, I don't think, because I just wanted to sleep with anyone I could get my hands on that I was attracted to. I wanted to make love. I wanted to make love right then. And when I was making love, somehow it made me feel more worthy. It made me feel that someone cared about me, even though, of course, that wasn't true at all. Instead of making me feel more worthy, it made me feel less worthy. Somehow there was a moment there of passion, of connectedness. I reached out to touch somebody and somebody was touching me back. And that wasn't happening at home. I wasn't feeling supported and loved at home. I felt like nothing compared to my brothers and sisters."

"Then what happened?" I asked.

I watched and made sure someone was helping the woman wading after the flamingo. She was still in the pond.

"I got my law degree, and I finally got married. I married a man who undermined and abused me. We had three children and still, I felt like I was not worthy of a good marriage. My parents had a wonderful marriage. If they fought, we never saw it as kids. So when I was fighting with my husband, I thought that, of course, I was not worthy of a good marriage."

The whole drama in the pond was going on behind my friends. I loved the surrealism of live swans, plastic pink flamingos, soaking-wet attendants, marriages come and gone. Our little dramas— where is our sense of humor? Even in the thick of it we have to learn to laugh together.

"In other words," Bev said, flipping her blond hair back from her face, "you mean that you have never felt at peace, then." Bev had been studying Buddhism for years and had the demeanor of someone who had meditated and done a tremendous amount of work on herself.

"Yes," Pat said, "I have never felt peace except in stolen moments in my life, when I would win an arbitration or actually help someone out of a nasty situation. I finally left my husband, thanks to you, Lynn. If you hadn't encouraged me and supported me in my dreams to live a better life, I could never have left him."

"Well, you did survive that, and you're stronger because of it. Now you're making a lot of money in your own firm."

"Yes, I am," Pat said, "but that didn't mean anything to me, so now I'm in therapy because I don't want to be sick anymore. And Lynn, we need to work together. We need to talk to each other more, because I need to be sure that my spirit stays as strong as my emotional and mental sides. I feel like I am empty, so very empty."

"How do you make it through every day? You must feel so terribly brokenhearted with your mother, with Bill."

"Yes, I do, but I work very, very hard. Every day I get a little bit stronger. Then, when I'm attracted to a man that I can see is dysfunctional, because that's all I'm attracted to . . . I know if some man comes across a crowded room to talk to me at a party that he is probably an alcoholic, takes drugs, or is dysfunctional in one way or another."

We all laughed.

I giggled as the woman retrieving the flamingo slipped on the rocks in the pond and went head first into the water, the swans hissing and attendants yelling for help.

"I can relate to that. I understand exactly what you mean," I said, shaking my head and remembering my own wedding and the mistakes I made because I was so nervous.

"Yes, so can I. I used to do that. I used to be so passionate about finding someone. It didn't make any difference about the relationship, I just wanted to be with a man. I wanted to be wanted," Bev said.

"That's exactly right," Pat said. "I wanted love, but somehow I was missing the part about respect. I was more into the sexual aspect of relationships. It was like being a man."

"You know, Pat, Agnes said something to me years ago that I think is true. I think maybe it applies to all women on one level or another. The earth is a female planet, whether you believe that or not. Just forget about what you believe for a moment, and hear what I'm saying."

I looked at Pat and Bev, who were framed by a fuchsia bougainvillea cascading down from the arbor above.

"The energy of the earth is female, and women have an innate understanding of that energy. Men, however, have to learn to adapt to the energy. They're male on a female planet. They feel like they are lost and that they need the woman, the goddess women that we are, to teach them how to live. I don't think this is a conscious thing. Don't misunderstand me. I think it's quite subtle. In our society women must struggle to maintain feelings of self-worth, and we often let ourselves down because we're afraid of who we might be were the men in our lives to leave. We're afraid to discuss the truth of our existence. When you don't feel worthy of the man that you're with, then what could possibly make you strong enough to teach a man how to live?"

Pat looked at me, her eyes confused. "When you say 'how to live,' do you mean how to act in life? What do you mean, exactly?"

"No, what I mean is how to live with a sense of purpose in life — how to balance the physical with the spiritual, how to have a life that is giving and loving, and yet is strong in ego success. A man has to learn that he does not have to dominate his mate, because she is whole and strong, perfected and balanced on her own.

"Isn't it interesting," I continued, "that we live in patriarchal societies around the world where women are dishonored, where women are unrecognized, where women are unheard, and yet we're the ones who have the responsibility to raise the children and to bring balance onto this planet, ecologically and between the male and female energies?"

"So, it's spiritual as well as physical?" Bev asked.

"Yes, I think that's right. It's not that men are less than women, or women are less than men. It's just that we have different purposes on this planet. So maybe it's possible, Pat, that when Bill asked you to be the goddess for him, you gave away your power."

"The thing that I found out to be most true," Pat said, tears in her eyes, "is that I made him the center of my universe. Instead of being the source of my own power and loving the peace and the joy and the experience of just being with myself, I needed to be with Bill or someone else to feel whole. If I didn't have Bill, I didn't feel whole. It was the typical example of women who love too much. And codependency. Looking for the source of my own power outside of me."

"The most tragic thing," I said, interrupting her, "is that you spent half your life giving away your power. I teach people to take their power back. I know about this because I've given away my power, too, in different situations in my life. Every once in a while, I get into a dilemma where I want to give it away again. Sometimes it takes me a couple of months to realize that I'm even doing it. When I realize it, it scares me because it can happen like a thief in the night. Someone comes in and steals your power away, and you don't even know it for a moment. Are you giving up power now because you're afraid of the unknown, the future?" I asked Pat.

"I hope not—no," she said emphatically.

We sipped our drinks, and I watched as the young woman, bedraggled and triumphant, carried the pink flamingo with its sopping-wet bow above her head. With help she climbed out of the pond only to slip on bird poop in the grass and land, flailing, on her back on the lawn. By now there was such a ruckus that everyone turned to look as the swans trumpeted and flapped their wings, and attendants ran to help from every direction. We looked at each other, shaking our heads in amazement, and laughed together. I had a sneaking suspicion that the young woman with the flamingo could actually be the bride.

TEN

She Who Walks with the Wind

In my home in Los Angeles I had decided to go up the path behind my house to meditate, looking out across the lush green canyon. I closed my eyes, reclining comfortably under an acacia tree. After some time I went deeply into a trancelike state. I no longer felt the humidity in the air or smelled the scent of roses blooming around me. Instead, I was transported by a wish, or an invitation, to go a long way away. I had been called into the presence of my old friend and teacher, She Who Walks with the Wind.

Her hands, strong and scarred from years in the wilderness and sun, trembled as she rolled the large crystal around in her palm and watched the light shift and brighten within it. This was her way of magic. She Who Walks with the Wind was a Hand Trembler, one of the ancient clan of seers. "She walks on the back of the wind," the old ones said. Edna, her familiar name, could see into other worlds through crystals and tell you the truth about things. She saw truth illumined on the rainbow prisms of light within the crystal's flaws. As a result, Edna could choose to do anything. She might tell you what she saw, grinning at you with her few silver teeth flashing in the sun, or she might choose to rise gracefully in front of you, watching your eyes, and say nothing. She might drift on the west wind, disappearing into the swirls of smoke from the camp fire, leaving you in wonder, or she could follow the voice of spirit and choose her death.

"I have called you because I have reached the end of my time," Edna said as I sat before her. The moon had appeared from behind a cloud. Suddenly Edna's footsteps echoed on the canyon walls, the shock of her unexpected appearance nearly taking my breath away. The cold wind whistling through the canyon seemed to follow her as she walked around me, her long skirt whipping her ankles and billowing in a white flow.

"Come with me," she said simply.

I knew that her work in our world was finished. She had passed down her wisdom. She had always said that when I had truly learned "the trembling" from her, she would go into spirit, other dimensions where her work was needed. Her life was a prayer, a gathering of knowledge and a giving away of her light to all who asked. She was a true seer—one who picks up the trail.

When I awoke, it was dark outside. I had curled up on my right side and must have been sleeping for some time. I got up slowly, brushing acacia leaves off my legs and arms, remembering Edna, the dream, and the sound of her voice calling me. Although I'd been home only a few days, I would leave the next day for Edna's home in the north.

The next morning I answered the phone reluctantly in the midst of my rush to pack, call a cab, and make my way to the airport. It was my mother's voice I heard, on the verge of tears, telling me, incredibly, that my stepfather, Jim, had been diagnosed with cancer.

"Mother, I'm on my way up north. One of my teachers is passing away. Would you like me to stay, because I will if you need me. Oh, Mother, I'm so sorry. Who's with you?"

"Vanessa is here," she said, and I was relieved that my daughter was there with her.

"I'll call you as soon as my plane lands," I said and hung up. I was numb as I sat in the back seat of the cab, feeling ill, as we wove through traffic.

It dawned on me that I couldn't possibly leave without seeing Jim and making sure Mom would be all right. I asked the cab driver to turn off the freeway and head toward Brentwood. I called and changed my flight to the next morning and arrived at Mom and Jim's apartment a half hour later. Geraniums, night-blooming jasmine, and bougainvillea spilled over their second-floor balcony. Vanessa, her long blond hair in a ponytail, answered the door and hugged me in surprise.

"Oh, honey, I'm so glad you're here," Mom said as we hugged and cried. My mother was five-foot-two, small and slight, with an unfailing sense of humor and an elegant grace about her.

Once we made sure Jim was comfortably settled in bed, the three of us talked late into the night.

"You know, when I met Jim twelve years ago, I knew that we would be married." This was my mother's second marriage, and she had met Jim late in life. They adored each other, raised flowers and orchids, loved to cook, and took long walks together.

"Mother, it's always so wonderful to watch you and Jim—your closeness, your respect for each other. It's so different from the way you and Dad were." I thought back on the nightmare of my early childhood, the fights, the yelling, the fear. "Mother, it must have been so awfully hard on you to try to raise me with no help."

"You know, Jim helped me get over that painful period of my life. I never cared much about religion, but Jim insisted that

I become a Catholic, and now I'm really glad I did. It's become a wonderful part of our life," Mom said, getting up from her chair and trying to hide the tears that had begun to well up in her eyes.

"Oh, Mom, it's so unfair," Vanessa said to me, her beautiful face stormy with tears.

"Jim is going to be okay," I said, taking her hand and Mother's. "Whatever happens, it is the way of spirit."

"He seems so strong and healthy," Mother said. "He's never looked better. We're so happy."

It did seem particularly cruel that the great happiness and peace my mother had found late in her life might now be taken away so suddenly.

We were sitting at my grandmother's inlaid wooden table that she had brought over by ship from Norway many years ago. My grandmother, tall, stately, graceful, and kind, had been so dear to me and had taught me so much. Who could imagine my grandmother, descended from English queens and the Nobel family, suddenly uprooting her life and moving to America where she gave birth to my father and my uncle? So much change! All of our lives have been like a surrealistic patchwork quilt of culture, education, poverty, love, abuse, and shifting mirrors of reality, each one reflecting great emotional shifts and threaded always with spiritual belief and music.

My mother too had been a fine pianist and possessed an operatic voice. She had been a celebrated dress designer. Now that was part of an obscure past. Her dreams and talents were hidden, it seemed, from others. The thought of this was tragic to me. Where had her dreams gone? Had she lost them because she had had to support us? My mother never talked about her artistic longings. She had given them all away when she had married my father, losing a whole piece of herself. I worried about her now. She had no community around her. Her friends and family were mostly gone.

For Edna it was different. A whole tribe of extended family would be with her. Love and respect had always been given without question to the elders. They were included in tribal decisions because their opinion was valued.

I ran my fingers over my grandmother's table, wondering how many times she had sat there, writing me her wonderful letters when I was living with my father in eastern Washington. Her letters had inspired me, as had my mother's.

My mother was watching me gently touch the table. We had become so close that she knew my thoughts. She reached out her hand and touched mine gently. Even at eighty she was still radiant and beautiful.

"Mother, do you want me to do ceremony for Jim? Will he let me work on him?"

"Honey, I think it would be a blessing for you to do ceremony. Jim told me that he wants you to pray for him. But you know how he feels about chanting and drumming and all that stuff."

Mother and Jim had never quite understood my brand of religion. My adventures frightened Mom because she thought I would be endangered in some way. She and Jim were happy with their religion, so I never pressed.

"I think it's best," Mom said, "if you don't talk with him about this. He has great faith in his doctor and his way. Lynn, darling, is that okay?"

"Mom, of course it is. I'm here as a healer and also as your daughter simply to make you feel better. I will pray on my own. And I do understand. I know Jim has great faith and draws strength from his Catholic beliefs."

Mother nodded as she got up from the table to check on Jim.

"Oh, Mom, I wish I could make things better." Vanessa came over, and we held each other.

"Honey, tell me what the doctor said today."

"He said they are going to try some procedures and some new medications that will give him, perhaps, a chance to go into remission."

"What do you think, Nessie? How do you feel about this?" My daughter had always been very psychic. The women in my family were very close and could read each other and those around us very clearly.

"I think he has time," Vanessa said.

"I'm going to send Mom and Jim down to Rancho Santa Fe to their favorite hotel so that they can enjoy themselves and have a second honeymoon," I said. "Nessie, can you make the arrangements for me? I have to leave in the morning. Did the doctor say Jim would be ill from the medication?" I asked.

"No," she said. "I asked him that, but he did say he would be tired."

"Are you going to be okay, Nessie? Do you need me here?"

"Mom, it's really okay. It's better if you're not around sniveling, anyway," she said, laughing and poking me in the ribs just like Agnes does.

My mother came back into the kitchen, blowing her nose, a brave smile etched on her face.

"Jim just woke up for a few minutes and said that he would see you in the morning. He's awfully sorry, but he needs to sleep."

I wanted to see him very much, but I didn't want to disturb him. He had been a strong, loving influence in all of our lives.

"He said he loved me," Mother said, looking wistfully out the window, her eyes looking so terribly sad. Then, Mother leaned over and gave me a big kiss and a hug and said, "Goodnight, darling." Then she kissed Nessie on the cheek. "Goodnight, sweetheart," and went off to bed.

An anger welled up inside me. I looked around the kitchen at the thoughtfully hung impressionistic paintings, a kitchen full of love and caring, and I wanted to break everything in it. I grabbed Nessie's hand.

"Honey, come on. Let's walk down to the pool," I said.

"What's wrong, Mom?" Vanessa asked, as we stomped down the stairs.

We walked out to the pool area and the gardens, hearing the rush of traffic on Sunset Boulevard even at this late hour. The air was scented with honeysuckle and jasmine, completely at odds with my bleak mood. I felt so furious that I squeezed Vanessa's hand until she had to pull it away.

"With all I know," I said, "I know nothing. I'm so angry, honey. I just don't understand sometimes."

"I know, Mom," Vanessa said. "It seems like all the good people die, one after the other. I hate it," she said. "I hate God right now."

And I was angry at the lousy hand fate had dealt to my family. "Why couldn't they live to be old?"

"Mom, they are old," Vanessa reminded me.

"Well, I mean really old," I said.

We laughed and cried together, but I was mostly angry. We walked out of the garden and down the street to the Catholic church, St. Martin of Tours. I tried the front door, and to my surprise, it was open. We walked into God's sanctuary, genuflected and crossed ourselves with holy water and seated ourselves very quietly near the altar where Mother and Jim had prayed so many times. I closed my eyes and thought of my years as a Catholic student, once again experiencing a flush of emotion and a sense of God around us. I prayed that this god, Jim's god, would rescue him. In my memory I could hear organ music and Mom and Jim's voices singing. I looked at the icons of Jesus and Mary and Joseph and wondered at the beauty of it all and the pain. While it had been many years since I had been in these surroundings, I still enjoyed being in silence, engulfed in my own sense of spirit and sacred thoughts.

In ceremonies with Agnes and Ruby, we all worship or call on holiness in our own ways. With Agnes, we wake up spirit with our chanting voices, dance, sage burning, and drumming. Here in this church, the voice, music, and incense were similar, yet so very different. The Sisterhood uses lodges sometimes for ceremony, but usually we are out under the stars, calling on their presence and power. But here, we sat in a house of God, serene and holy. God had always been inside me. Even as a young girl, I had been moved by the beauty of the icons, the light from the votive candles, and the prayer inside my heart. The holiness lived inside me and always will. I thought of Jim, and I knew he was praying. I sensed him in my mind saying that I had time to go north, but not for long.

When we finally left, walking softly down the aisle, we lit a candle for Mother and Jim. Light is light. Flame is flame. We were stronger and our hearts were more buoyant when we left the church.

In the morning as we gathered for breakfast, I finally got to see Jim, and he was surprisingly chipper. I could tell that he was hiding his anxiety from Mother, but he knew that I could *See* him. I saw the darkness around his throat and lungs. Jim and I stared at each other for some time, and I looked deep into his soul. I gave him all the healing energy I could find. He felt it, knew it, and simply nodded to me in recognition. I wanted to ask him to please let me work on him. Silently, he just shook his head. His answer was no.

"Did you go to church last night?" he asked.

"Yes, it was open," I said. "Isn't that unusual?"

"Yes," he said, "but I am so glad that you were there."

We talked some more about Rancho Santa Fe and finalized the plans for their trip. Before I left, I told Vanessa to have the hotel fill their room with flowers.

All the way to the airport—swerving through traffic, honking horns, the cab driver yelling at irate drivers—I was surrounded by a cocoon of fog. I was joyous about the passing of She Who Walks with the Wind, because I knew it was her choice and her time. Perhaps it was Jim's time, too, but why did this feel so shocking and untimely? I was deeply stunned. My reactions were so confused that I couldn't sort them out. I was happy for Edna. I would miss her, but I knew that I would still work with her in spirit. She might even appear to me in the physical. She had that ability. Choosing her death seemed peaceful and correct. Jim, however, was dying at a most unfortunate time. Mom and Jim in their separate ways had prepared carefully for their retirement years. Perhaps that's it, I thought. Retirement is a strange concept if you love what you do, and even if you don't, at least you keep busy, focused, and useful. I had seen this early in my life. I had walked away from a lifestyle that didn't support my yearning for spiritual work. I knew that it was my destiny. I also realized that I could write and work in the healing arts even if I lived to be very old. Most shamans are very old. All of my thoughts didn't help my frustration. I couldn't fix this situation, but I would make it more comfortable for them. I would pray for Jim and help him to see his beloved family waiting for him just on the other side.

ELEVEN

Choosing Your Death

In just a few short hours I had arrived at Edna's log cabin—light years away from Los Angeles and the other world I knew so well. Edna and I walked down a horse trail near her home. She looked thin and drawn, clear evidence of the state of her failing health. We piled her modest furnishings into the back of a pickup truck and set off down the gumble road.

I took a right turn and headed down toward Penelope's cabin, where Edna was going to drop off her rocking chair. Everyone knew that Edna was choosing her death. Penelope was waiting for us on her porch. I stayed in the truck as Edna talked with her friend a short time, hugged her, and said good-bye. Then we went on down the road toward Indian John's place.

Edna rested her hand on my shoulder as if to talk, so I drove slowly to avoid the ruts in the road.

"Long before this day, I decided to immerse my life in spiritual teachings. I wanted to make my Tree of Dreams full and strong," Edna said in her quiet, gentle voice.

I let her words sink in and then replied, "Now I too am looking at my own elderhood with a sense of wonder and even passion. It is the passing of life force that people are afraid of, but this fear is wasted because our life force never dies!" I said. "All my teachers and friends like you believe that the animation of power becomes greater as you grow older, not lessened. I feel it, Edna—that's our agreement with the Great Spirit. Why do so many people believe that as we get older we must lose power?" I could see Edna struggling to stay lucid and help me understand.

"Sometimes I send away my spirit helpers to purposefully become vulnerable to the mountain winds. I feel the air as if it were my beloved, and I want to live there in it, blowing across the earth. I have to give away my knowledge and skill to become fresh, in order to see the rolling currents of life form meanings that I have not yet realized. I become my essence. I am the inside of any form that surrounds me. Many people feel this way when they die, and it is all left behind in a dream. But the Tree of Dreams never dies. It blooms again in another season.

"When two people are in love, one person's heart can change the rhythm of the other's. That happened with my husband," she said with a faint smile on her face. "But now, people live with almost no song in their hearts. Our hearts seldom beat as one. We're not intimate enough.

"In the West, many in your society are approaching elderhood, and they seem to be filled with anxiety and confusion about their future. However, we are unique individuals in each of our societies. I've always found wisdom in my crystals and strength from my creativity, so I see elderhood as an approach of higher wisdom and respect for the poetic soul in each of us. I don't think that is how all people see life, though. I wish they did. For the most part, people seem to need comfort and distraction from any real confrontation with the undercurrents in life. My life is my work of art. I am a spiritual woman like you, an artist looking always for my expression. But to *See* is much more difficult than to express. To *See* the undercurrent is to approach dreams and your subconscious with open arms, allowing the subtle essence of your existence to become visible. Feelings of fear and anger are healed only by an understanding of your creative soul.

"This is what you have always been able to see, black wolf. This has allowed me to go on my way, and I thank you for it. My heart is full."

We rounded the turn in the road, and Indian John's cabin appeared in front of us. He also was waiting, standing in the driveway.

We drove over the countryside that day, and one by one all of Edna's things were given to her dearest friends. Ceremonies had been done. The bridges had been crossed. Those who knew her were respectful, they were honored, and while some were sad, they all felt a celebration in their midst.

When the time came, She Who Walks with the Wind returned to her cabin and finally lay down on her bed, the only belonging that she had kept except for a tiny gold cross. She reached over and put it around my neck.

"This is for your Jim. He will not mind a cross. It is good."

As I sat on the floor next to her, it began to rain, and we could hear the raindrops on the tin roof and the thunder above. Zigzags of lightning split the sky. I held her hand, and we talked about her memories of people that she loved. We spoke about her adopted children. We spoke about her husband who had passed away long ago. We talked about her path of sacred medicine and how it had been both difficult and joyous. She had learned and shared so much about magic and the mysteries of life. As I sat with her, I understood more clearly that life and death are merely different sides of the same shield. Death is a process of beginning, not a process of ending. In death we wake up from the dream.

I held her hand, and She Who Walks with the Wind slowly began to let her spirit fly. She breathed deeply, then looked at me one final time. Smiling gently, she closed her eyes. I closed my own eyes and moved my attention into Edna's departing dream. She was moving into the spirit wind. It swirled around us as I joined her momentarily for one last farewell. She showed me the swirling colors of the wind currents as she moved toward home—shields and beads and crystals—all of her totems and ancestors surrounded her. After this magnificent experience, I walked outside the cabin leaving her inside and watched a stream of sunlight coming from the horizon. It was so bright and vivid that I felt as if I could follow it into other worlds. For a moment I thought I could see She Who Walks with the Wind moving slowly toward the mountains as the sun went behind the horizon and a strong wind came up from the west. After praying, I turned to go back to the cabin, and I was startled by what I found. Only ashes were left on the bed, except for Edna's sacred crystal. I knew she had left it for me. Edna had self-immolated, a bright flame now reflected only by the smoking mirror of immortality.

TWELVE

In the Wind

The experience of Edna's death was so powerful that I needed to share it with someone, so I passed through New Mexico to be with my teachers. Agnes and I sat beneath giant cottonwood trees near the Pecos River, where we had been camping for several days. We were talking about Edna, who had chosen her death only a week before.

"Agnes, I feel her all around us. I feel her in the reflections of light from the river. I feel her talking to me in the wind."

"What is Edna saying to you?" Agnes asked.

"I think she is telling me that she is always with us, that she has gone on to other dimensions, but she will return," I replied.

A breeze came up from the east, and the cottonwood leaves danced in the sunshine. The sounds they made were so beautiful and tender that they brought tears to my eyes. I could still see Edna as if she were sitting with us, talking about the joys of her life, talking about truth and her willingness to give her attention to my soul.

"I hear her, and I feel her, Agnes. She is powerful."

Agnes took several minutes as she whittled on a cottonwood stick, making the figure of a kachina, a thunder spirit. Finally, she said, "You see, when there are great teachers in the world, they are involved with many, many people. They are involved with the spirits of so many in their process of enlightenment. When they choose their death, they move on into the world of spirit. They move on into spirit, but they also visit us because of all that they have witnessed. Edna was with us on this level for so many years and I hesitate to say how many."

"Oh, Agnes, tell me," I interrupted. "I've always wondered."

"No, but let's put it this way. She lived through the old ways and she remembered many things. That means that she had been here for a very long time before she chose her death. You can imagine the people that she touched."

"She is here to take care of them?" I asked.

"Not to take care of them, but to watch over us."

"So she may be here for a long time?" I asked.

"She may stick around for many months, even years, depending on what her purpose is."

"Her purpose?"

"Well, she had a great destiny in life. First, she knew the discipline of Hand Trembling. She became a seer. Therefore, she could help others down that trail, as you know. To become a seer in any tradition requires insight and support. She is here to give you that. She tends to your luminous fibers, or the energy field around you. She clears your fibers of negativity and watches over you with great care. That's why you feel her. So she may be here for a long while. You may feel her for years."

When I got back to Santa Fe that night, I called home to check on my mother and speak to Jim. "How is the medication going?" I asked him.

"Good, but it's making me very tired, as was expected. Now they say I've not only got cancer of the esophagus but of the lungs, as well."

"How could this happen?" I said. "I'm shocked. You look so wonderful."

"You know, Lynn, I can't tell your mother this, but I need to tell somebody. I keep thinking about something that happened about a year ago. This strange man came into the laundromat and tried to rob us. He was the oddest-looking fellow."

"What did he look like?" I asked.

"He was an Asian man, and his eyes were so fierce they terrified me. When I stopped him from taking the money, he looked at me and said that he'd be back for my soul. His words were so startling and went so deeply inside me, I'll never forget it. You know, I honestly believe that he had something to do with my illness."

"Jim," I said, horrified, "what a terrible experience! But you know as well as I do that if you believe something is true, you will make it true, even if it is not."

"Yes, yes. But it was a very disturbing experience."

"In a sense, Jim, you must not let fear change your life. It sounds as if you didn't respond to that event—you just reacted to it. Please, Jim, try not to let that happen."

"I know it's ridiculous, but I can't get it out of my mind," he said.

Just like I couldn't get Red Dog out of my mind, I thought. It was impossible to get Jim to change his mind once it was set, and I had a feeling this time wouldn't be any different.

"For now they say I'm in remission. Now I simply do this awful waiting, but it gives me time to be with your mother."

"I love you, Jim, and I'm praying for you. Sometimes we have the capacity to make ourselves well. Please try, Jim. Please stay positive."

I talked to my mother for a long time afterward, and finally hung up, exhausted.

That night Agnes and I did ceremony for Jim until morning, when Ruby joined us for breakfast. Then they sat on either side of me to show their love and support. I was overcome with grief and fatigue, but as I relaxed, and we shared our thoughts, I felt invigorated and loved.

THIRTEEN

The Trickster

Agnes, Ruby, and I decided to move our camp to the east side of a small natural spring, and there we sat, leaning against an outcropping of boulders that had tumbled down from the crest of the craggy granite hills around us. The rocks looked like marbles collected by a prehistoric giant. A twisted piñon tree shaded us from the sun. We sat in the dirt feeling the rhythms of mother earth beneath us, each of us in our own way. I felt a gentle breeze on my cheeks and watched the play of light across old Acoma ruins standing like jagged sentinels guarding us to the east. The air smelled of grasses and juniper bushes and fresh clean space. I took a deep breath, filling my lungs, and relished the quiet that surrounded us. Agnes and Ruby sat with their eyes almost shut, as if they were going to nap, something they often did while sitting bolt upright in the sand. Agnes finally broke the silence, and I began to dig frantically in my pockets for a scrap of paper and a pen.

"You are thinking about words, little wolf. You know the power of words. When I tell you a story, there is not only the story, but there is the process of listening to that story, so I don't want you to use your writing words right now," Agnes said, and I laid the paper down to listen.

"But Agnes, you have said this to me before—that I would always remember stories when I needed them. But what I miss in trying to remember these stories is the subtlety behind your words. I have always written what you have told me. I need to have those details, otherwise I can't breathe life into this process that you and I have always had together."

"Ah," Ruby said, "that is truly the point, Lynn. The story is only one aspect. The listening is the most important part because of the swirl of the air, earth, water, and fire. How you listen to a story and what that story actually gives to you through the wind on your face and the light in your hair and the feel of the earth beneath your feet, all of that comes together in the sharing of any living information."

"What is living information?" I asked, since this phrase was very unusual for her.

"You become aware. You can see the life in all the named and nameless things," she finally said, just as a butterfly landed on the very top of her head. She smiled, her eyes picking up the reflected light of the sun.

Our attention suddenly turned to a rustling noise in the bushes below where we sat, peering across the small clearing, and wondering who had joined our circle. A pair of glittering eyes watched us from underneath a juniper bush. I looked again, starting to get up, but Agnes held my arm and kept me on the ground. A moment later a coyote, a female, nosed her way out of the bushes. She sat proudly at the edge of the clearing, her paws shining and well cleaned, her toes gently dug into the surface of the sand. She looked at Ruby, cocking her head a little to the side. I sat in wonderment, keeping as still as I could. I had never seen a coyote behave in this manner. Agnes slowly turned her gaze from the coyote to me. She stared into my eyes for a very long time, as if in a trance, and I began to see pictures in my head—pictures of words with big letters, like *mountain* and *sky*, and then little words next to them, like *honest* and *lies* and *beauty*. I was transfixed by the power between us. I dared not move or breathe lest I break the spell. And then a story or a procession of thoughts marched through my mind.

"The coyote will trick you," said a voice in my mind. "The coyote tells you to beware and to examine even those that you trust. Long ago, little wolf, you were told that all must be balanced in this world, the male and the female, the earth and the sky, the mind and our feelings, spirit and the physical. All of this is true. And then you were told to find and take back the marriage basket from Red Dog. He was dangerous and meant you great harm, as you well know. He had stolen the marriage basket, a great ceremonial medicine object, because he needed its balance and power. He needed the female powers it carries. Stolen or not, it would give him this power. The coyote is here to tell you something. She knows of Red Dog. She knows. Listen to her, for she has a tale to tell."

I looked slowly, carefully moving my eyes and then my head to look at the coyote who was now pinning me with her jasper-and-yellow eyes, her attention completely fixed on me. I felt like prey, frozen as a deer caught in the headlights. My heart started to beat irregularly. I wasn't sure that I wanted to hear this tale.

"Red Dog has chosen to stay on the earth. He has changed his ways, but he still lives on the dark side of a sacred altar. He chooses the monastery from whence he came long ago, and he dreams your dreams. He loves you still."

My eyes opened wide because I had never imagined Red Dog loved anyone, least of all me. No, it was hatred I felt from Red Dog.

"He loves you and gives meaning to your understanding of the light," the coyote told me. "He celebrates the Great Spirit even though he lives in the shadows. I warn you, little wolf, that there is much yet to be learned about your own power and weakness. You are afraid in your relationships. You are afraid that maybe you will lose your way. You are afraid that you will lose your song. That will never happen, but beware, little wolf, for there are forces at work that you have yet been unaware of."

"He's not out to get you," Agnes joined in. "He's out to destroy the power of the elders. He wants nothing more than to take their power for himself, but he is seeing that his old ways don't work. You showed him that. He is on the side of the dark angels, but even the dark angels are connected to the Great Spirit, as is everything. We're hoping and praying, just as we did for Sin Corazón, our great apprentice who fell prey to a dark sorcerer. We pray for Red Dog, as we do for anyone, that he can find his way without harm."

"Red Dog has visited me in my dreams of late," I said, "but I thought his presence was merely a symbol of my own fears and my stepfather's illness. I can't believe it's really Red Dog!" Hearing about Red Dog from my teachers was a powerful warning. I was aghast. My heart pounded in my chest and I stared at them in disbelief. "You mean to tell me that Red Dog is still alive?"

They glared at me, and then I realized that I was being disrespectful of the coyote, this beautiful female who sat watching me with quiet disdain. I nodded to her as if to an elder, honoring her. A moment later I heard more scurrying under the brush. The coyote lowered her head, her ears softening for a moment, as five little pups came out to join her. They seemed to take position next to her—three to her left and two to her right. There they sat, just like their mother, paws in front, little heads held at attention. I couldn't help but smile at their beauty. The clouds that had been gathering above us parted, and the sun shone almost directly overhead, warming the afternoon.

Inside my head I heard her again. "These are no ordinary pups. These are the pups that represent your incubation."

I was startled at this strange word and flashed my eyes toward Ruby and Agnes. They shook their heads for me to pay attention. They had heard the words as well.

"You are learning, little wolf."

"Why a coyote?" I wondered in my mind.

"Because I'm a trickster," she said. "I can test you to see if you are true."

She turned on her haunches, nuzzling her pups, and disappeared under the bush without a sound. They were gone as suddenly as they had appeared. I didn't know if they had been in the spirit or in the physical form.

"Were they . . ." I started to ask, but Agnes and Ruby laughed. I knew I would have to discover the answer for myself, just as I had for most of the questions I had ever asked. My teachers have always wanted me to find the answers on my own through experience.

"The elders," I began again, "why does Red Dog want to take power from the elders?"

"Because they know the stories," Ruby said. "They know the stories that inhabit this world. Stories must be heard. Stories must be told. Your story, little one, is a different one. It's a different kind of story. Your stories are about your spiritual growth, but you have shared these stories with a world that is unfamiliar with them. You must translate. You have grown along with these stories and helped others to grow. You have helped others to see in the mirror of your experience. This is part of your song. You are working with the elders. You love the elders and you always have."

Tears flowed down my cheeks as I looked at my elder teachers, still feeling so naive even as new recognition dawned on me. I looked briefly again toward the bush, all spines and scraggles and thorns, wondering how animals survive at all.

Then I remembered something that they had said to me so often. "Don't get caught in the dream," I said. "That is one of the parts of this story that needs to be learned. As people grow old, they actually become more awake—they learn a new reality. Their consciousness is a magnificent bridge between that world and ours. Yet we ignore the elders and demean them because of the change in their physical appearance and ability. We must learn to see them differently. I am very honored that I was able to hear the story and also that I truly listened to it without distraction. I see what you mean, Ruby. If I had been writing, I may have missed altogether what this story was trying to tell me."

I gave thanks to my teachers for their love and knowledge and also to the coyote family for their story. I took a strand of my hair and offered it to the spirit on the wind.

Time When

the Trees

Blossom

All the truth
She Who Walks with the Wind says,

dances in the center.
I am only this shadow

dreaming this body awake.

Mind is not the healer
yet one must heal the mind.

In the east,
a schizophrenic woman saying,

my love is my disorder,
my disorder is my love.

FOURTEEN

She Who Walked Before You

Later that week I went to an Acoma ruin to reflect on all that had happened. A favorite spot of mine, the ruins occupy a mesa high above the desert floor. As I sat in the crimson evening light reflected on the ruins, I wondered about the lives of people who had come before me a thousand years ago. I ran my fingers over the surface of a crumbling wall, wondering if perhaps another woman ages ago had sat there just like me, musing about the truth of things. I prayed for guidance as I thought about Jim and Edna, trying to understand the meaning behind disease and death. I wanted so much for my family to live on forever. I thought back to my two failed marriages, the problems I'd had raising my daughter, and my relatives who had passed on. I was still grieving these things—still missing my family so. In life there are so many little deaths, and as they happen the challenge is to understand the meanings and teachings that are there for all of us.

I rested my head against the sandstone wall and closed my eyes. The sun had just dipped below the horizon and I began to dream.

The owl sits on the eaves of the portal, calling those who are asleep into the Tree of Dreams. The memories of my life flip by—those things that brought me here when I was lost in a world of clanking dishes and fine crystal, the sounds of children crying, the dishwasher, the dryer in the laundry room with a pair of tennis shoes flipping around on the heavy dry cycle. Lying on sheets with no one touching. Lost days with no one speaking. The world is full of talking, yet no one listens. Our hearts beat, but we don't reach out. Loneliness, and yet there is God that fills your chest. My chest was full of love and light, and yet the yearning to wander, to discover, to identify, to reflect what I was feeling went beyond my control, and I couldn't stop. Courage had moved into another place in my body, into my soul instead of my guts.

Nothing could stand in the way of my touching the face of God with my tenuous fingers even though I knew not what they were searching for. I thought it was God, but I kept getting in the way of God. All the messages were there.

The dishes could have waited. The sounds might have had a different meaning. The music somewhere in the distance could have filled me, but I never allowed it. Was it my unnamed addictions, silly distractions? Who knows? Was it written, Agnes? Could I come to you and only you as the messenger from the divine? You called it shamanism. I called it my relationship with spirit, and it filled me . . . The holes that I felt still reside someplace within me, but I don't want to admit that they exist. Often people who know of God refuse to admit that the more they know, the more the knowledge seems to define their extraordinary ignorance.

I came, Agnes, because I could not live where I was. I came to you because I saw the light in you. I saw the humor, the kindness, the compassion, and the beauty. I yearned for beauty. I yearned for the great north wind on my skin like silk, welcoming me into the sacred dream where I met you and held your hand. I followed you. It took great courage to change everything in my life to be here. And yet, now I see that nothing really changed except my perspective. I found the ability to allow something new to grow inside me, a child of wisdom and God. An awakening to the unrecognized one, the one who is never heard, the one who was hidden and denied. I was all of that, my white skin now sunburned and dark, unknown to those around me. But the changes within me meant that I could be heard and recognized after all and that the risk to be of service was never too great. I had to share what had been gifted to me with all the love and the caring that I could find within my own heart.

What I know of you now, Agnes Whistling Elk and all of you in the Sisterhood, is that you live for prayer, for divine awareness. You are in communication with the masters that have walked before us, the teachers that have stood like the great trees among us, offering example and perfection. You are forever in service to the light. You have led me out of the darkness. Before, I would diminish what I knew. I would ignore what was in my own heart and spirit to please something less worthy. I misplaced my compassion time and again. Perhaps that was my addiction.

I felt a presence near me in the darkness, a shadow, sweet and tender and kind. I heard a voice speak very softly, almost like the sound of the wind. It was the voice of the woman who had once lived here.

"Dear sister, we have walked before you. Our footprints live on in the pots that we formed and in our dreams. I was just like you, sister. I worked in the far away, and I worked in the world. I was a seer, and I was a woman of song. We did ceremony too. And we taught each other, like the wolves teach their pups. There was much that was sacred in our people.

"Long ago, we had trees. We had a Tree of Dreams like yours. I will take you to the Tree of Dreams that resides in your heart. The Tree of Dreams represents truth in your life. Do you see it there, shining in the moonlight? It is a symbol of our closeness to spirit. The roots move down

into the earth, strong, beautiful, gathering nourishment as they reach to the core of mother earth. The Tree of Dreams embodies the spirit of the great mother and is enriched by the great sky fathers, rain and sun. . . .

"This Tree of Dreams is all that we are. When our leaves fall, they are golden and beautiful. They carpet the earth with memories of our lifetimes. Lie down in those leaves, dear sister. Wrap yourself in the memory and grieve with your whole heart and soul, and then let your grief blow away, like leaves on the wind. Be done with it and never look back. For us, the Tree of Dreams was cut down, and we lost our way. Our trees no longer stand, but their roots are still in place beneath the earth. And now through the love in your heart, we live on and the Tree of Dreams lives again."

Then the voice was gone, and only the sound of the wind remained. I opened my eyes and allowed the healing tears to flow freely.

FIFTEEN

A Reckoning

When I returned to camp that evening, I sought out Agnes. Our camp was made up of three cabins that resembled hogans. Large old ironwood and palo verde trees shaded the camp from the afternoon sun and silver sage dotted the desert landscape. Quail, coyotes, deer, and javelinas came through on a regular basis. A temperamental creek ran behind the old hogans, which had been patched numerous times, and I could see in the beams where pieces of wood had been hacked out and new logs inserted. The adobe walls were different colors. Some looked blue from the content of mica in them, and others were dark brown. At night in the firelight, the walls of the hogan sparkled like so many stars falling to the earth. It was beautiful, and I could almost hear the ancient voices in the walls.

Each hogan had a porch, or portal, equipped with *latias*, which are thin round logs. Latias are laid across larger beams, called *vigas*, which hold up the structure. The portal on our hogan was old, but it served us well when there were many of us gathered around. Most of us slept outside under the portal, which was also shaded by large, old trees. One very old cottonwood danced in the wind and provided music to lull us to sleep.

The next morning I woke up late, feeling groggy, as if I hadn't really slept. I tried to write for several hours without much success and decided to take a walk late in the afternoon. Nothing felt right about that day. The air lacked its usual clarity. I noticed strange shadows and I kept tripping. I should have gone back to the cabin, but instead, I kept on walking, hoping the exercise would do me good.

Out of nowhere a dust devil appeared from the winds that had been blowing through the chaparral. I thought I saw Red Dog standing between the curves of the rocks ahead, but then the dust devil dissipated and the vision was gone. It had been my imagination. I stood there for a long time before walking over to the crevice where I thought I had seen him. There were no footprints, no stones out of place, nothing that spoke of his presence, but a chill had enveloped me.

I walked around the boulders, and again, a dust devil came up from the ground. This time it swirled around me, covering me with fine dust and pieces of dried grass. I brushed myself off, amazed at the suddenness of the wind. Abruptly, it was still again—deathly still. I sat down in the middle of the path and listened for the birds, but there were none. A thrill of excitement ran through me, and I knew something was happening.

I sat for a long time, placing protection around me. Rocking back and forth on my heels, I sang my power song and waited.

For a third time, the wind picked up and urged me down the draw. Three crows flew overhead, cawing, warning me. I rounded a corner in the wash and ahead of me, standing on a low ledge of red rock, now unmistakably, was Red Dog. I was startled, thrilled, and horrified, all at once.

Tall, thin, dressed in black flowing vestments, Red Dog was an imposing figure. Perhaps this is his ghost, I thought, but he began to speak to me as though we had been comfortably conversing for hours.

"I seek to defy you," he said, towering over me. "I seek to destroy your history. I seek to plunder the legends and the stories that you hold dear, because they give you power. They give you the resilience and the endurance to defy me," he said.

How dare you, I thought, as I stared at him, transfixed. I was fascinated by the crucifix that hung around his neck, the white priest's collar that dug into the skin below his chin. The sun streamed down through the dark gathering clouds and bounced off his crucifix, creating a dull luminosity that had been hidden under years of accumulated tarnish on silver. I was astonished by his presence, for I had not seen him in many long years and had never expected to see him again. I stood there dumbfounded, taking in his darkness, wondering how or why the Great Spirit would give life to such a person.

"Why have you come?" I asked, finally.

"I have come to you many times over the years. You simply have not seen me," he said. "I have hidden from you in the shadows, enjoying the game, playing with you like a cat plays with a mouse."

I was outraged by his rudeness, his incredible presumptuousness. At the same time, I began to notice a change in him from when we last met. He was stronger somehow. He seemed well defined. He was ominous, and yet he exuded a certain vulnerability — not a weakness, but rather like light around a thunderhead. It gave him the odd quality of being accessible, which I had never felt before. He seemed seductive in a way that disarmed me. I had the feeling he possessed knowledge and skills unknown to me, and I grew curious at once. I wanted to know what had made him pick the dark, empty road of a sorcerer.

He smiled for the first time and cocked his head like a crow. "Ah, I knew you'd be interested," he said. "You've always been curious. I knew danger would attract you."

I smiled very superficially, but then I had to agree. "I consider my curiosity to be an asset. Whether I'm kissing the stars or hugging the dirt in the road, I always learn something. I must admit, I have been curious about you. Why would you deliberately choose to hurt people, to be evil?"

He laughed uproariously at this. "Evil? Indeed. Did you ever stop to think that evil may have chosen me? For every act of creation, there is an equal act of destruction," he said.

"You and I have been good enemies," I said, "but we have never had a chance to talk. We have haunted each other into the depths of our souls, but in a certain chaotic way, I believe we have defined each other. So why have you come back? Haven't you had enough?"

The wind picked up from the west, cold and blustery, swirling around him. How fitting, I thought, as he held onto his black cloak with a nervous flutter of his hand, revealing his worn laced boots. "You have just explained why I have returned. In fact, I never left you, and I never will. I own you."

I had to laugh at that, almost snarling at him. "Nobody owns me or anyone else for that matter," I said.

"We'll see about that."

Red Dog walked down the trail a bit further and disappeared behind an outcropping of sandstone boulders.

"Come," he called.

I was about to turn and go in the other direction when he repeated, "Come. It is sheltered back here and we can talk. It is time."

How like Agnes that sounded, I thought, but then I realized he
had picked up mannerisms, intonations and even words from
Agnes to trick me into his web. With this in mind, I followed my
curiosity and joined him behind the boulder. Sure enough, he had
found a sheltered area, a long ledge of rock circling around to the
right. With plenty of distance between us, he sat facing me in what
looked like a confrontational position. I sat across from him and
narrowed my eyes to focus my *Seeing* ability on him. I could see energy around his navel from where the spider web of power em-
anates.

"I have been in a self-imposed sanctuary," he began. "My path
was illuminated, but in a different way than it has been for you.
You live only in the light. I create a bridge, and I walk between the
light and the dark. I do not believe that there is anything that is not
created by God."

Red Dog observed me, his face more deeply etched with lines
than when I had seen him last. He was clean-shaven, and this was
the first time I had really seen his face—white and nearly transpar-
ent. The lines around his mouth were cruel and austere, his eyes
piercing, but I thought I noticed a fleeting sadness. Sadness was a
vulnerability that he would not show me. I watched the energy
around him and noticed that the spider web of power near his navel
was missing several strands. I wondered if they were missing because he was hiding something and did not wish me to see him in
any truly meaningful way. I felt his contempt for me, and I knew
nothing that I said to him would affect him.

What a profound experience to have the opportunity to sit with
this man who had been my adversary ever since the beginning of
my spiritual practice. This man had threatened my life, and had

even stolen the soul of one of my dearest friends and trapped it in a gourd. I have never understood how this happened, but I know that it was a fact. With my own eyes, I witnessed the event as he stole the spirit of a beautiful young woman named July. With her spirit held captive, she appeared to be dead to us—wandering the wilderness, as if insane. We feared we had lost her forever. Only when Red Dog released her did she come back to life as if she had awakened from a long dream. Red Dog was not one to play with, and I knew it. I knew that this priest was now an even more devious and powerful man, whether he was dark or light. He was a sorcerer of great intelligence and skill.

"Why do you hide behind the dark side of the altar?" I asked finally. "What could you possibly gain?"

"Everlasting life," he said, pausing and watching my astonishment. "What you don't understand," he said to me, "is that I am playing with you. Everything that I say to you is a lie. You know that you can never quite figure out who I am, and that's the ultimate seduction for you. You will live for that. You always have lived for that. As far as you're concerned, that's the most important thing in the world—maintaining interest and curiosity. Boredom is death for you. If someone were trying to kill you, boredom would be his best weapon." He laughed. "So I have, excuse the pun, dogged you, all of your spiritual life. I've been in the background of your mind. Do you remember when you were in Nepal and Tibet? Do you remember your terror?"

I looked at him, but said nothing. He had my attention, however, because it was true. I had gone through a period of terror, being so far from home, far from everything that I knew, in the foothills of the Himalayas. I was surrounded by superstitious people, fierce healers who misused their power to frighten me. They told me that I was being haunted by a dark sorcerer, and of course, the first person I thought of was Red Dog. It was then that I learned of his death, and I began to transform my fear into the understanding that enlightened people with true power do not use their skills to destroy. During this time, I had met a woman named Ani from the hills of Chepang. She was also a member of the Sisterhood of the Shields. Over buttered tea one afternoon, she talked to me about the eminent scientist Albert Einstein from my own Western society.

"He meditated and studied his whole life," she said. "His work in mathematics purified his soul so that finally he was gifted with extraordinary power—knowledge and the theory of relativity. At that point of revelation and the attainment of true power, he knew he would never use these gifts to destroy another human being."

I realized then that while the mad sorcerers of the world have certainly harmed people out of ignorance, people of real power would not use their gifts in this way.

But now, here was Red Dog, once again before me. His power seemed to crackle in the air. He was full of trickery, illusion, and seductive charisma.

"Devotion of a brighter kind is lost forever within the mind," he said in a singsong voice, laughing.

I sat there wondering in amazement that I was having a conversation of any sort with Red Dog. He was alive and he was right here before me! Red Dog was a fascinating man, but a terrifying personality at the same time. At times, he even looked like a holy man, but he was anything but.

As billowing dark clouds gathered above us, casting slow-moving shadows over the rocks, Red Dog suddenly changed his demeanor.

"There is so much pain in the world," he said.

"Yes, why would you add to it?" I asked, feeling gray inside.

"People receive in this life only what they ask for."

"But surely we do not ask for that kind of pain. Did July ask to have her soul taken? Do you really believe that, Red Dog?" I was chiding him.

"Yes, I do."

I didn't answer.

"We all need to grow," he went on. "That's all this life is about. If I add to someone's pain to get what I need out of life, then so be it. I enjoy it and it gives me power. Pain will come from somewhere, so what does it matter if it comes from me?"

"Even if that means killing someone, I suppose?"

"Yes, it does. Killing them just helps them transform." He yawned then and stretched as if suddenly bored by our conversation. "Let's have an exchange of wits," he challenged. He stood up and moved around the circle, holding his crucifix in his right hand, smoothing his long black garments with the other.

"What a strange apparition you are," I said, thinking back to a time years ago, when he had embedded a turquoise bead in my leg in his attempt to control me and destroy me. "I remember you in the Polo Lounge in Beverly Hills, dressed like a gentleman. What a surprise it was to find you leaping out of the wheelchair that you had used to make your entrance! I hardly recognized you. You are a master of disguise. I honor you for your great skills. There is no question that I recognize your power."

"I have never been able to hurt you," he said, "because you don't hate me. If only you had hated me!"

I looked at him, not wanting my eyes to convey the true contempt that I had for him. And yet, inside me, I could not hate him. He was right.

"I understand that we all must walk this earthly plane so we can learn to transform into greater awareness," I finally said, the wind beginning to whip the sand that had gathered in the crevices of the boulders and stones tumbled around us. The scent of rain was in the air. I took a deep breath, centering myself, trying to settle my pounding heart because I knew that I was in great danger. I knew this discussion was inevitable and I am sure that somewhere it had been written. We were fulfilling some kind of strange prophecy between us—the light defining the dark, the shadow self of woman and man in discussion with that part of us that is light and full of spirit.

If you look deeply into your life, you will see that in each moment you die a little, because you change or grow. The beauty of each moment is in the birth or the death of some aspect of your experience. How can you hate someone for disliking you or even wanting to hurt you? In your compassion, you see their pain—you see their struggle. You may choose to fear that person and avoid them, or you can learn from them.

"I have lived with fear and I know that you have too, Red Dog. You choose your horse in life, so to speak, and then you have to ride it."

He stared back at me. I had no idea what effect my words were having on him, but I knew that he was paying attention, because I was still keeping him guessing.

"I have been eating you alive," Red Dog said with a big smile on his face. "I have been using your strength. Because of your love for wisdom, your wonderful wisdom," he taunted me, "I have been able to access your vulnerability. I have found your holes and have been able to put my power into them. At times you have found yourself doing things that you wouldn't ordinarily do, saying things to your friends or acquaintances that you couldn't explain."

I thought back to a few instances where I had really lost my temper, only to wonder later what had gotten into me. I'd had to apologize profusely for my behavior afterward. I remembered other times, too, particularly in the last year, that I couldn't explain, when I seemed to enter another identity. I hadn't seen it that way at the time, but now I realized that somehow I had given over to a kind of possession. I stared into Red Dog's eyes, and whispered the word, "Possession?"

"Possession?" he snarled, leaning back against a stone. "That's not what I would call it, but close enough, you silly woman. When are you going to see that you are responsible for what you feel? There is no such thing as possession. It's all God."

I looked at him, not knowing what I wanted to say at this point, because in part I agreed with him, but I didn't want to have a discussion of ethics and logic and philosophy with Red Dog.

"What's the matter?" he asked, reading my mind. "Are you afraid that your logic won't hold water?" he said, taunting me. "This body is an illusion," he said, patting his chest. "You are lost in a maze that you think is the light, and you think your path is goodness and what you call God. But God is powerful—all powerful, and God will take whatever he wants. He knows how you want to be told what to do."

"I do not want to be told what to do," I blurted out. I couldn't stand his taunting anymore.

"Well, there are many who do, many who need guidance every day, and many people get fooled. They think they are speaking to the light, but they're not. They are speaking to the dark angels."

"People know the difference between the dark and the light angels."

This sent him into fits of laughter. "Oh, you are so naive," he said. "How do you know the difference between the light and the dark? Evil often looks like good. It is very tricky. You see, Lynn, it is not revenge that I am looking for, even though you have embarrassed me in the past. You actually outwitted me, although I hate to admit it," he said with a sly smile. "When you took the sacred marriage basket away from me, you almost killed me. You stole it back, but now it is not revenge I am looking for—it is a reckoning, a reckoning at the highest levels of spirit, of heaven and hell, and the forces of nature."

I stared at him for a long time. A palpable silence had formed between us.

"A reckoning? A balancing?" I asked. "A reckoning, indeed. How could there ever be a reckoning between us? More like an apocalypse, I'd say. How could two generals discuss their strategy before going into war?" I stated with intensity.

"Well," Red Dog said, "I suppose I could kill you, because in the language of sorcery, you killed me. But I came back to haunt you, and I will continue to do so. What is of highest interest to me," he said, "is returning the powers of nature to their proper perspective. I have come into your dreams many times," Red Dog said, glaring. At the moment, I felt very confused, because I knew what he was saying was partially true.

"I have seen you in my dreams," I said, "but you cannot control my dreams. You will never do that."

He studied me but kept absolutely still. The wind had picked up and swirled around him again. This time I looked up to see an owl swoop down from a scrub ironwood tree clinging to the side of the cliff. The owl soared out of sight, but the sign that she had provided for me had not gone unnoticed. The owl sounds a note of caution in some cultures, or that death is near in others, or she is a symbol of wisdom in still others. To me, the owl is a warning to pay attention. I believe great beauty and great wisdom come with owl medicine, but still, she is an awesome warning. This wise old owl came out of her home on the wheel in the east and she flew toward the west, the place of transformation, death, and rebirth—a sure sign of warning.

Red Dog and I began a dance of good and evil, a dance of light and dark, an exchange of psychic energy. We moved around each other, positioning ourselves, trying to find the warrior's corner—that place of power. But neither of us could find one, because there was none. A place of power is where you find strength, where you have a vantage point. It's like being in a room with your back against the wall. But there was no wall to find here between us. We were evenly matched and so we danced. We watched one another. We were enormously careful of each other. I could see that he had, perhaps, changed. I could see that now more than ever this dance was important to him, that somehow a formidable enemy gave him life. We were of no use to one another beyond this dance.

Just then Red Dog reached into his pocket. He took out something and threw it on the ground in front of me, and said, "I made this just for you."

I looked at the object more closely and jumped back in fright. There at my feet lay a dead lizard with a blue belly and a long shiny tail. It had died with its eyes opened, and it stared at me in its eternal silence. Its mouth had been sewn shut with red thread.

"Now you can't lie to me," Red Dog said.

I knew I was in danger now—this was a powerful symbol of his magic. I stared at the lizard for several moments before turning to look at Red Dog, who had walked off to my left. For a moment, silhouetted against the setting sun, he looked for all the world like a reptilian demon from another reality. I thought I saw protrusions on his head and tiny sharp teeth in a gaping, evil smile. His eyes were no longer human, but absorbed the light like dark holes in the earth. He made a sudden movement, and the vision disappeared.

It was a ghastly moment the likes of which I'd never experienced. Perhaps it was my imagination, and the light was simply playing tricks on my eyes. I stood there in the awesome glow of the sunset, staring at him. He took the lizard and put it back in his pocket.

"The lizard was already dead when I found him," he said, winking at me. "But his message should be clear—we must tell the truth."

My mind felt confused and cloudy. What had just happened here? I thought to myself, still uneasy. Red Dog seemed gentler now, as we continued our conversation.

Before today, I thought that our war was over, but Red Dog was right. A reckoning was upon us. I knew he meant to scare me, and I felt strange. For a moment I wondered if this was his cry for help. He seemed to be looking for something, a visionary part of himself. He was hiding something. The spider web around his navel never became whole. A chill came over me as I realized that this experience was like a dark form of Spider Woman's medicine.

"Perhaps it seems chaotic, but I am weaving a fascinating shimmer of ideas to intrigue you, ideas about life, survival, death, invisibility, mystery," he said.

He was skilled at maneuvering his body language to entrance me. I had jumped into his web of mastery with my own free will. He had enticed me through my own hunger for knowledge.

"You're like Eve and her famous apple. You have taken a bite from what you saw as light, or food, for your soul. You are staring at the mouth of your own destiny, a destiny that has been repeated by you over and over throughout lifetimes."

"I am already whole and complete," I said.

"No, you have looked for distractions and magical experiences outside yourself to find love," he said.

"Could you possibly be doing the same thing—looking for a source of power outside yourself?" I asked emphatically. "The deepest love comes from the Great Spirit, and I already know what that is. My source of love is not outside me, nor is it inside anyone else."

He said nothing, but moved around with extraordinary grace, as if in a dance. A scent of sage was in the air, and my thoughts and attention began to meander into the pictures he was sending me — scenes of tribal peace and beauty, and a golden glow of light. For a moment I felt a powerful, heavy force, as if I were under Red Dog's control. I wanted to leave but I could not. All I could manage was to sit there, mesmerized by Red Dog's visions and his strange dance.

Suddenly the feeling was gone. He had stopped and he turned his head slowly to observe me, and I was free. He smiled with knowing eyes, walked around a huge boulder, and was gone.

SIXTEEN

Trust Your Seeing

I could hardly contain my fury as I ran down the path back to the camp. I had to find Agnes right away, and with each step closer to finding her, my temper flared higher and higher. It was all making sense now—all the pieces, the little jokes and hints she shared with Ruby, my dreams. They must have known all along that Red Dog was coming.

I found Agnes sitting underneath a blooming palo verde tree, hands in her lap and eyes cast to the sky, as peaceful as could be.

"How long, Agnes, did you know that I would be seeing Red Dog? How long had you known without telling me?" I yelled, stomping around in circles, raising little puffs of dust with my feet.

"Only a very short time," Agnes responded with a look of patronizing kindness on her face. She knew more than anyone that I had been dealing with my fear of Red Dog for years. "I have known for a couple of months."

"Is that all?" I demanded.

"Yes, but there were several of us who knew he was alive, including Spider Woman. She saved his life."

"What?" I sputtered. "What!" Instead of my anger dissipating, I was now in a rage. "How could one of the Sisterhood . . . that's just outrageous . . . what . . ."

"Something outrageous? How could I have missed that?" Ruby asked, sitting down next to Agnes. "Nice to see you mad again, Lynn. What's the commotion about?"

"You! All of you! Spider Woman! Is that why she was getting close to me? All of you! You've left me out. You've betrayed me. Did you save him so he could kill me?"

They couldn't hold it back anymore. The two old women started to shriek with laughter.

"I'm glad you think this is so darned funny. This has scared me out of my wits, and you've hardly prepared me."

"Since when was that our job?" they said in unison.

I sat down on a rock in a fit, suddenly deflated, not knowing what else to say.

Ruby looked at me, shaking her head, "Temper, temper. I want to tell you a story, Lynn, that you might find interesting. It's about something that happened to me and has meaning for you."

She paused a moment, running her fingers along a stick she was carrying.

"Picking mushrooms is hard. You have to be like a mushroom yourself to find them under the pine needles in the forest. Just like what you see about yourself now—the truth, like the mushrooms. It was there all the time. You just didn't see it."

I stared at Ruby, thinking to myself, "This is another one of those lessons I'm missing." I said nothing, but somehow I felt a little bit better. Maybe it was her words. Maybe it was just the sound of her voice, but I calmed down a little.

"We could see Red Dog in the dreamtime," Agnes said. "He hides himself very well, but at times he would let down his guard, and we could see him. I knew that there would be a reckoning between the two of you. There was no other way."

"Oh, great. What do you mean, there was no other way?" I asked.

She thought for several minutes, tracing her fingers in the sand, touching the granules gently, as if she were touching a memory deep inside herself.

"There is a violence that has always surrounded Red Dog," she finally said, "and that violence is something that held him back. It was a block, a limitation to his power."

"No, kidding!" I said. "So what does that have to do with me?"

"You were the object of his anger many times, as we all were, but he knew as he went through the gateway of death and returned that we could see this in his energy field. With that transition, some light returned to him."

"Lightness in Red Dog?" I asked in amazement.

"Yes," Agnes said. "Even Red Dog is capable of lightness."

I thought about that for several minutes as Agnes observed me intently. I took a swig of water from my canteen and set it down in the sand.

"In other words, you are saying to me that he began to heal and that light came into him, finally, that he allowed it."

"Well, yes," she said, "but he also learned that he had to pay a price—we pay a price for everything."

"There's no free lunch," Ruby added, laughing.

"You see," Agnes continued, "Red Dog is a sorcerer. A sorcerer is usually born out of greed and envy. Control is an essential element of his life. In that process of controlling everything around him, there also occurs a stasis, or rigidity. If you become solidified—solid in your belief structures and in your techniques—there is no fluidity. Remember? Just like that river we stood in. There is no ability to bend, to curve around something the way he needed to in order to own it. So he started losing power. That's why he needed the marriage basket as a female symbol. However, it never would have been enough, because he had to become that marriage basket. He never could do that, so he tried to steal and take power from others. And then his life was taken. But it was given back to him through Spider Woman's sacred songs."

"Wait a minute, wait a minute," I said and started pacing back and forth. "Oh, my God, you mean the dream I had was for real? That really happened?"

There was a silence. We just stared at each other. I felt as if the wind had been knocked from me, and I collapsed down in the sand where I stood.

"What you dream is real," Ruby said.

"How could you not have realized it?" Agnes asked very quietly.

I started drawing lines in the sand with a stick, saying nothing, as my life began to flash in front of my eyes. Thoughts of New York, Jim, a kaleidoscope of colors, sounds, pictures of Red Dog years ago in his tin-roofed cabin, the marriage basket. I took a deep breath, trying to find my center. Like a cloud blowing across the moon, something shifted inside me, and I was still again.

"Trust your *Seeing*, Lynn," Agnes said. "Red Dog was given the song. He needed to return the song to Spider Woman within a few hours, which he did with honor. But he could never be what he truly wanted to be. So, like a good sorcerer, he decided to do something about it. He became a survivor. He returned to the monastery where he came from, and he went into spiritual hiding. He covered up his essence with great skill. He unearthed the ancient teachings of immortality. But in the meantime, he had to become creative. He learned quickly and filled the void within himself with creativity, and that took away his anger. As you know, violence is healed through creativity, just like chaos, and his energy field began to look different," Agnes said.

"So that's why you didn't see him for a long time," I said.

"Yes, that's why we didn't see him for a long time. The chaos around him changed, and he ordered things differently, so we did not recognize him."

"Could he ever really change, Agnes, and become a good person, a truly spiritual man?" I asked.

"Of course he could," Agnes said.

"But he probably won't," Ruby chimed in.

"Why not?" I asked.

Ruby tilted her head to one side, thinking, chewing on a twig. "I think his whole life seems to be about stealing power without taking responsibility one way or another. I would be very surprised. That is just my sense, but I would be very surprised," she said.

"But that's strange," I said, "because we have always had hope that no matter what, someone will find his way and heal."

"Yes," both of the women said.

"But you asked me a question and I gave you an answer," Ruby finished.

"Okay, okay," I said, "don't get mad. I just wondered."

"Sometimes," Agnes said, "you simply get lost in the darkness, and that is your path for this lifetime. That does not mean that you cannot heal. Our sister, Sin Corazón, healed and has become more powerful in the pursuit of wholeness and light than she ever was before. So it can happen. It's just our opinion that he is a very dangerous man.

"As you have seen before, Lynn, tremendous darkness still surrounds him. There are holes in his armor now, but he's still hiding a great strength. And there is only one reason that he would hide — he doesn't want his evil to be seen. The more he hides, the more dangerous he becomes. He may look as if some goodness lies beneath the surface, but he is now more dangerous than ever because you want to see him as healed. We all do."

SEVENTEEN

Sacred Fool

Agnes and I took the low trail through a dry river bed back to the hogan.

"West wind is blowing for you, little wolf," Agnes said.

I searched the red cliffs above me, trying to read the shadows for some sign that might enlighten me. A red-tailed hawk settled into her nest in a deep slash in the stone surface and disappeared except for an occasional flurry of movement.

"I'm so filled with emotion, Agnes. Why do I still have such confusion and anxiety about Red Dog?"

"I wouldn't call this confusion and anxiety," Agnes said. "I would call this an obsession."

"You've said that before. Are you right—I haven't changed in all these years? But I don't feel obsessed with Red Dog ... Am I?" I slumped down, feeling confused.

"You sleep on that," Agnes said. "In your dreaming the answer may come."

She was right, of course, and now I was eager to let sleep overtake me. I strung up a hammock between two trees as the others prepared for the night. The camp was soon asleep, and as if in answer to my prayers, I began a shaman dream.

Face in the Water stood up in my night vision. I had never seen her move so abruptly. She had my attention. She looked into my eyes for a long time. Then slowly, she walked around me, touching my shoulders and hair and then the top of my head, brushing her fingers like a whisper of wind gently blowing over me.

"You can't change your original nature," she finally said. "You can't lose yourself and go so far astray that you can't find your way home. It's not possible."

The sun began to set on the horizon. The wind eddied around us and cottonwood leaves chattered and shimmered in the quaking orange light of my dream. Face in the Water's brown skin seemed to melt into the shadows, and I blinked, but a thick mist surrounded her. Just as suddenly, she lifted out of the shadows on huge wings, her face a beak, with piercing eyes. She had transformed into her power bird, a condor in flight in pursuit of her dinner—me.

"You are on the edge of a precipice into which you desire to leap." I could still hear her voice talking to me from far away. "Are you throwing everything away that you have learned? Of course you are. I am a carrion bird. I clean up the waste you create in your learning. I could tear you to pieces right now. I could pluck out your eyes, so that you could see only with your soul. I could tear out your heart, so you could no longer love. Is that what this is about? If you leap now and finally understand your relationship with Red Dog, does who you've become or what you are die?"

"Yes," I said, staring at her ominous presence looming above me. Suddenly I was so afraid, not only of her, but of myself. Flapping her huge wings, she reached out and grabbed hold of my index finger with her beak. I yelled from the pain as blood began to run down my hand. "What do you want?" I screamed.

"I want you to stand in your power even as you leap, you fool. To be alive you must risk everything—only in death are you secure. You have always been the sacred fool. I have picked up the trail behind you for all these years. Now you listen to me, black wolf. You cannot lose who you are. People get mixed up with things, but you are like a tree. You are mixed up with nothing. Like a tree, you are on your own—firmly rooted and secure in who you are. Accept it. There is no other way. Go ahead, jump, you fool! It's all you can do, don't you see? You learn now to risk it all, and you must or you will lose."

The pain in my finger was excruciating, matched only by the pain in my belly. Gliding on her wings, the great condor disappeared into the shadows of the night, leaving me shaken and bleeding. I awakened suddenly out of my dream and sat up in the hammock, considering her words about risk. Did she mean follow my obsession? I thought a long time and finally decided that this was a dream about feeling alive. I couldn't back away from Red Dog. I would risk being in his presence. I might even challenge myself on every level of being, but I would not step out of my own sacred circle of power. To me that was beyond risk—it was foolish.

Time When the Leaves Turn Gold

Spider Woman
teaches us

all much more
all much more

all much more
singing.

More
mystery

of the cactus and the rain.

The old men of the desert,
full of the desert,

this is the rain falling on the earth.

O thanks
O thanks be

and all much more
singing.

EIGHTEEN

Death Is an Ally

I awoke fairly late in the morning, and although the sun was already up, the vision of my shaman dream was still brilliant in my mind. I looked at my finger to inspect the cut, but there was none. For some unknown reason, instead of being inspired like I always was by my dreaming, I had plummeted into despair. I knew that not all dreams bring joy and that the teaching can be painful, but I didn't seem to have the energy to care.

As I lay in the hammock, I heard one of the women rattling. It sounded like the old mother rattle, but it soon stopped. I lay still in the unmoving air. Rattle, rattle, rattle came the sound again. Why were they rattling now? I thought to myself. Then a chill ran through my whole body. The sound was coming from underneath me. Carefully, I rolled my eyes, turning my head ever so slightly. There it was, coiled up, right underneath my head, on the ground below! A huge diamondback rattlesnake with a darting tongue and ten rattles ringed in black and white. His eyes stared straight into mine. I lay there frozen, then looked away, not wanting to confront him. I was afraid to breathe. We were caught in a stalemate for some time. The rattling continued, but he didn't strike. I began to pray to his spirit.

Startling me, Ruby, pushed through the screen door of the hogan and slammed it behind her.

"Great Spirit, please save us. What are you still doing asleep?" she yelled at me, stomping her moccasinned feet toward me and creating a stir of dust.

Then she stopped dead in her tracks, instantly aware of trouble. Without a further sound, the rattlesnake uncoiled and slithered away into the underbrush. As I lay there recuperating, Ruby stood over me.

"Did you hear the rattlesnake?" I asked. "There was a rattlesnake underneath my hammock," I said, finally allowing myself to breathe.

"Sounded like Red Dog to me," she retorted, hands on hips.

"What?" I asked, getting up.

"Better be more careful," she added, walking into the hogan. She slammed the screen door again, which was something she never did.

I followed Ruby into the hogan and basked in the welcome relief of filtered sunlight and the cool air inside.

"I feel almost as if that snake bit me," I finally said to Ruby, sitting across from her. I swigged coffee to no avail. My vision was veiled and slow. Even I wondered about the snake and if Red Dog had sent him. Of course he had, I thought, scaring myself all over again.

"You can't be creative when you're in denial," Ruby said.

"You're feeling dull because you're off your center," Face in the Water said, sitting down with us. "You don't want to face the fact that people you love can actually pass away. We don't live forever, but in another sense, we do. This has to do with your fascination with Red Dog."

My eyes still felt cloudy and half open. All I wanted to do was sleep.

"I'm not fascinated with Red Dog," I snapped.

Face in the Water pulled her chair over next to mine. She looked directly into my eyes, put her hands on my shoulders and shook me. "You know what it really is?" she asked.

"What?" I asked sleepily, as if drugged.

"Like all human beings, you are fascinated with eternal life."

"Eternal life? Are you saying that Red Dog might live forever?" Now I was awake.

"Lynn, you know about us. You know that we are much older than we seem. You are drawn to this. Whether you know it or not, you want to know the secret."

I mulled this over for a long time, sipping coffee. The fogginess cluttering my brain came and went like a drug-induced stupor. I couldn't seem to shake it altogether.

"You are torturing yourself. Feeling dull is your will trying to wake you up and your conscious mind attempting to keep you asleep. You are fighting so hard against it. It's your nature. This is a lesson."

"What's my lesson?"

"You're fighting your own will. You need to give up the fight. Your obsession for Red Dog endures because you think he's a cat with nine lives."

"How is it that Spider Woman can sing him back to life? My God, that's some song!"

"Right now, everything is about life and death for you."

"If Jim dies, why can't she sing him back to life?"

"You do know the answer to that," Agnes said.

"Yes, it has not been written as it was for Red Dog," I said.

"That's right," she said.

I sat down, holding my head in my hands. "I want us all to live forever just as we are."

"But we do live forever," Ruby said, rejoining the conversation and sitting next to me. I noticed she had tied deer rattles around her ankles. They made a beautiful sound like rushing water. "You're afraid of death, Lynn," said Ruby. "Strangely enough, in your relationship with Red Dog, you're finding the end of that trail. Our lives are inspired by the Great Spirit. You're beginning to see beyond a shadow of a doubt that the more light you have, the more life. Death serves to bring things sharply into focus. You have moved in and out of this focus all of your life. It has charted your fate. Now you are taking the feathered quill in your own hand and beginning to write your own story."

NINETEEN

Tunnel of Light

That night I fell into a deep, dreamless sleep. Early the next morning I went home to my rented house in Arizona and worked on my writing until late in the afternoon.

The phone rang, and even before I answered it, I knew it was my mother.

"Honey, you need to come home," she said. "Jim has taken a turn for the worse and is in the hospital."

"Oh, Mom, why didn't you call me?"

"It just happened last night."

Mother was crying and I was, too.

"Mom, I'll leave for the airport now. There are flights every hour."

"I'll pick you up," she said.

"No. Is Vanessa there?"

"Yes."

"Send Vanessa."

Two hours later I was flying toward California. The sound of the engines lulled me into a deep reverie. I was thinking of Jim and praying. I remembered a conversation we had had years ago. Jim was telling me about an experience he and his mother had had that had changed his life forever. Even in the telling of it, he was terrified, his eyes wide and tearful.

A woman, statuesque and quietly ascending the burnished wooden staircase of her home, reached out with her delicate hand. Her son had recently returned with a degree from Oxford and a newly acquired taste for English spiritualism. Neither of them could ever explain exactly what happened next, but the moment lived on in their terror-stricken memories forever. They reached out to hug each other and say good morning in the early sunlight that created a golden shine on the polished wood floors. The room was suddenly encased in shadows, and the sun disappeared like blood soaking quickly into dry sand. The stairs began to shake, wood screaming against nail and screw. A force, unnamed but immense, entered the house. Their eardrums nearly burst with the pressure in the air and the sound. The woman and her son were thrust against the wall. An otherworldly roar swirled around them, and then as if hands had formed out of the thick gloom, they were both shoved uncontrollably down the stairs to the landing below. His mother was unconscious with a broken hip and a fractured arm. Jim, her son, looked up at the high windows reflecting a demonic face of evil and eyes that glittered with a yellow intensity. A voice, growling and filled with malice, invited Jim to join him in hell. "I will have your faith," it said, and was gone.

There was a jolt, and we were landing in Los Angeles. I met Vanessa on the street at the baggage entrance. She leapt out of the car, and we hugged each other for several moments. It was so wonderful to see my beautiful daughter.

"This is so much for you to be going through, Nessie." I touched her face with my hand. "Are you okay?" She looked exhausted and strained.

"Oh, Mom, I'm so glad to see you." She started to cry, and I held her for a moment.

"Is Mom holding up okay?" I asked.

"Yes. Come on, Mom. Let me get your bags, and I'll tell you everything."

Mother, Vanessa, and I sat around Jim's bed in the cancer ward of the UCLA medical center. The lights were bright, shining off white cotton curtains. A man three beds away was fighting for his life. He had been in a car wreck. I couldn't imagine why he was in a cancer ward. Machines blinked and beeped, phones rang, the sound of gurneys echoed down the halls as nurses rushed in and out yelling for equipment. Howard Stern was on the radio behind the nurse's station. A child wailed in the waiting room. It was bedlam.

Jim lay quiet in a morphine-induced sleep. Mother held his hand, and I held hers, while Vanessa rubbed Jim's feet. We were waiting for the doctor. Mother was becoming frantic as Jim's breathing became more and more difficult.

"Where is the doctor? Where is the doctor?" she yelled. I put my arms around her.

"I'll go get him," I said. "Please relax, Mom. I'll find him."

An hour or so went by. I couldn't find the doctor. By the time I returned, Jim was in terrible pain. A Nurse Ratchett came to the foot of the bed. "If you don't calm down, you'll all have to leave."

"I don't understand why you can't give him more pain medication," Mother said.

"This is so awful," Vanessa said, sobbing.

I was standing next to Jim, trying to figure out what to do for him. I had closed my eyes and prayed. His energy was so scrambled from the drugs and the noise that I couldn't reach him as I wanted to, but I was able to calm him down a bit. By now another hour had passed with no doctor, no help, no pain medication. I walked out to a central nurse's station on the floor. A young man, belligerent and uncommunicative, stared at me.

"Are you a nurse?" I asked.

"Yes."

"We need pain medication, morphine, whatever you're giving him at bed 127 in the cancer ward."

"You have to talk to the cancer ward nurses."

"They are busy with an emergency," I said. "But I'm letting you know, right now, that *this* is an emergency! And my stepfather is going to have whatever pain medication he needs, and you are going to help me, right now!"

I reached across the counter with both hands and grabbed his white coat and pulled him halfway across the counter. I focused all the energy and the power I had into the eyes of this insolent young man. He said not another word as I let him go, but he jumped onto his feet. He straightened his jacket and went for the medication and gave it to Jim without even so much as looking at me.

Jim eased back and relaxed as the medication took hold.

"Thank God," Mother said.

I said, "Yes, thank God."

I held Vanessa and Mother in my arms. They were both terribly upset and crying and confused. There was still no word from the doctor, but he had told Mother that he would be on his way.

I closed my eyes and went to Jim's consciousness. I heard his voice.

"I'll be fine," he said. "Thank you. I see my mother. She is standing in a tunnel of light with all my family, and they are waiting for me. You take care of your mother. Prepare yourself, Lynn, for she will be joining me soon. It is all okay. I understand. The evil I was so afraid of is not here. How foolish that I was so afraid! I could have conquered this, but it's okay now. You will be okay. Vanessa—she is very strong. I will wake up in an hour to say good-bye. Please, tell your mother."

And then his voice faded away.

"Mom, Nessie, Jim has just told me that he will wake in an hour, and he will talk to us."

"He promised he would never leave me," Mother said forlornly. She kept repeating herself, her face so beautiful and sad. I knew she was in shock, and there was nothing that I could do but love her.

A priest arrived as the nurses rolled away the man, now covered with a sheet, who had been in the car wreck. He was gone. The priest gave Jim his last rites as the doctor arrived. The doctor took Mother out into the aisle to speak to her alone.

"How did this happen so quickly?" I asked Vanessa. "I thought things were under control for now."

"He had to go in for an emergency operation last night. He was bleeding internally. We tried to reach you."

"Oh, God, Nessie, I'm so sorry. I should have been here. I'm going to miss him so much. I can't believe this has happened so fast. It's so unfair."

The priest shook our hands and was gone. Vanessa and I looked at each other and shook our heads.

"Where's the doctor?" I asked Mother when she came in.

"Oh, he's leaving."

"What!" I went running down the hallway, calling his name. "Dr. Johnson!"

He turned and waited for me.

"For heaven's sake," I said, "you could at least talk to us and tell us what's happening."

"Your stepfather is dying," he said with no expression on his face.

"Surely, you can do better than that," I said.

"Last night he had a . . ." the doctor said, ". . . complications. I sewed him back up. There was nothing else I could do."

"How long does he have?" I said, after staring at him in disbelief.

"An hour, maybe. I'm sorry." He shook my hand and left.

I ran back into the room. Mother was not doing well. Her face was tragic. Jim stirred in the bed, and like magic, his eyes opened, and he came out of the morphine with amazing clarity. He reached out for Mother's hand, and they talked for ten minutes or so about how much they loved each other.

Suddenly, another bed was being rolled into the ward with two attending doctors. An old gentleman had just had a heart attack. Again, there was bedlam—beeping, phones ringing, people rushing in and out, clanking, hysterical sobs from another woman behind the curtain.

Jim reached out his arms and gave me a hug and then Vanessa. "Pray for me," he asked of us. "I love you so much. Take care of your mother."

And he was gone.

Suddenly nurses were surrounding the bed trying to help, finally, now that it was too late.

Mother was screaming at them, "Get away! Get away!" I put my arm around her, but she just wanted to be alone with him.

We closed the curtains and Nessie and I sat outside in the aisle. I thought of Edna and the peacefulness of her cabin and the joyous love that we had shared at her passing. If only I had been able to do that for Jim. I vowed to do something so that no one has the experience of dying amid such chaos. What a different experience this could have been with a little effort, education, and caring.

TWENTY

More Light

It was one of those fabulous California nights, scented with honey-suckle and night-blooming jasmine. I arrived at Doug Clantin's house just past eight o'clock for one of his intimate sit-down din-ners. I hoped I looked elegant in a simple, short black dress and heels, but my grief-stricken mood was in direct opposition to the spirit of the evening.

"Lynn, darling, you must come to dinner. Let us take care of you. I want to tell you everything," Doug had said over the phone.

I had agreed, although I wanted only to be alone in the wilder-ness doing ceremony for Jim, but Mom, Vanessa, and I had to see the lawyer in the morning.

I parked my car on the quiet tree-lined street in Bel Air, went to the great red-lacquered gate, and rang the bell. I was greeted by barking, snapping, snarling, and more barking on the other side of the gate, as a woman in a white uniform opened it and ushered me in. A two-story fountain of tumbling rocks and water loomed above, creating a fine mist in the air around me and the artistically designed pool at the front of the house. I walked up the stairs with five dogs—tiny silken terriers—sniffing and growling and yapping at my heels. At least they had learned not to bite.

Leaving the dogs behind, I walked into the living room upstairs. The onslaught of high white walls, light, the staring faces of the dinner guests, the string music from the cello and violin off to the left, and Doug careening toward me across the room made me dizzy, and I almost fell backward. Doug kissed me on both cheeks in his European way, thrust a vodka tonic into my left hand and grabbed my right elbow to steady himself. He led me around the room, introducing me to the Morrisons, Ann and Ron, a handsome couple, whom he described as art patrons and collectors of Picassos and Calder mobiles.

"One of the finest collections in the world," he said.

"Yes, you must come see them, Lynn. How nice to meet you," Ann Morrison said. "I've read your books. So sorry to hear about your stepfather."

We walked over to the long white sofa underneath a magnificent Monet painting.

"I would like you to meet Dr. Pillsbury, Timothy Pillsbury," Doug said. At this point he was reeling from the double martini he was sipping, probably the fifth of the evening. "Since you're a shaman, Lynn, and a healer, I thought you would enjoy meeting Tim. He's one of the heads of St. John's Hospital, internal medicine or something like that."

Dr. Pillsbury looked at me with a bit of skepticism hidden under his smile. "I'd love to discuss alternative healing," he said.

I nodded, thinking to myself, I shouldn't have trusted Doug to take care of me. I knew that he had invited this doctor just to argue with me, like he often does. He loves to pit one political candidate against another or one religious belief against another. I once saw Doug throw someone bodily out through his big, proud red gate into the street. Why do people put up with him? Because he's interesting, educated, and rich. I put up with him because we'd been friends since long before he became an alcoholic.

Then there were the Simpsons, a couple in their seventies. John was a retired investment banker who handled Doug's money, and his wife, Margaret, stood by looking uncomfortable, stuffed into her white dinner dress.

Lorraine Azure, the actress, was next.

"Lorraine is a Broadway actress. Surely you saw her in *A Chorus Line*," Doug said.

After saying hello, Lorraine, in green chiffon, swished across the Sarouk carpet and seated herself next to Dr. Pillsbury. At eight-thirty on the dot Doug's manservant appeared at the opening of the high Chinese screens at the end of the room and announced that dinner was served.

We entered the dimly lit dining room. The long glass table was sparkling with candles, silverware, and dragon-china plates from what looked like the Ming Dynasty. A ten-foot-tall polychrome golden Buddha held court from a corner of the room, surrounded by candles and flowers and soft oriental rugs on the highly burnished wood floors. The Buddha was from Doug's meditation days, now long forgotten. Only the art pieces remained. In the lit niches surrounding the room, pre-Columbian vases and sculptures of unestimable value stared out at us.

There we sat, Doug at the head of the table, I to his right, Dr. Pillsbury to his left, Lorraine to the doctor's left, the Morrisons next to her, and the Simpsons to my right. The music ensemble joined us, playing softly at the end of the room under the Buddha. At Doug's house the main course was always served first and salad last. The servers began to flap though the swinging kitchen doors, holding large silver trays of magnificently presented beef Wellington and duck à l'orange.

"Good grief, Doug," I said, "this is gorgeous," as I placed small servings of whipped mashed potatoes, honeyed carrots, asparagus, duck, and beef Wellington onto my plate.

"Good grief is right," Doug said. "I hope you're feeling better, Lynn."

"I am, thank you," I answered.

Then Doug stood to offer a toast with one of his best Rothschild wines.

"In Goethe's dying words—*more light*," he said.

As he sat down, I stood briefly. "For our wonderful dinner and to our host—continued life and health."

"How gracious of you," Tim said, looking at me across his heaping plate of food.

For several moments we ate in silence. My mind kept racing back to gourmet dinners cooked by Jim and my mother at their apartment and how lovely they were. I took a bite of duck à l'orange and thought of Ruby and Agnes and me eating beef jerky and sipping coffee by a campfire in the far north.

My reverie was broken by Doug, not allowing, ever, more than a few minutes of silence.

"Well, Lynn, what have you been working on, besides transformation and that highly overworked word, 'enlightenment'? Frankly, my dear, all that meditation I did never got me anywhere."

"Nice statue, though," Lorraine said, chewing on a piece of beef and dabbing at her lips with her napkin, leaving a slash of red on the white linen.

"Actually, Tim, I'd like to ask you something. My stepfather recently passed away from cancer."

"I'm so sorry," he said.

"Thank you," I answered. "Some people say that cancer is a virus. Do you agree with that?" I asked him.

"Yes, actually, I do," he said.

"May I speak to you about viruses for a minute?" I asked.

"Oh, God, do we have to talk about sickness?" Doug said, pouting and sloshing his drink onto his plate. "I really do hate to be sick," he said.

"No, no, go ahead," John Simpson said, adding a large dollop of mashed potatoes onto his plate.

"I'd like to hear this, too," Margaret said, her chin glistening with a drop of gravy, which she was carefully wiping away.

"I don't want to talk about health and illness," Doug reiterated.

"I know, but let's talk about the virus for a moment anyway," I said, ignoring Doug, who was getting very drunk. "The virus is something that has no energy of its own, right?" I asked, and Tim nodded. "It has no ability to reproduce itself, so it needs to find some sort of complimentary host to survive. In other words, it goes into something, like your body."

"Yes, and that is the beginning of infection," Tim said.

"So if that is true and you really think about it, a virus does not want to kill anyone, I don't believe. That's just my sense. It does not want to even harm anything," I stated.

"I'm going to harm someone if you don't stop," Doug said, ordering more beef Wellington.

"But, Lynn, it wants to do more than just survive, it wants to change. It wants that part of itself that is missing. It wants to become something else," Tim said, as he cut his duck into small pieces.

I continued, "So when I look at a virus as a symbol, I see that it is like the consciousness that has become a big part of our lives these days."

"How do you mean?" Tim said.

"Oh, God, all anybody talks about is cancer. I want to talk about life. How about you, Lorraine, how's your sex life?" Doug slurred.

"It would be better if I saw you more often." She smiled, as the candlelight reflected off of her beautiful high cheekbones.

"Well," I continued, "we're all trying to become something more. We strive to understand the greatest truth. So many baby boomers are hitting that age, Tim, where they're saying, *What am I going to do with my life now? Something is missing in me.* They still want to evolve. Perhaps they've worked their entire lives to succeed at something, raise their families, have their relationships, and so forth, but they haven't found fulfillment. So in wanting to become something else, to find that missing piece, isn't that symbolically just like a virus?" I asked.

"It's a matter of magnitude. We're both virus and the host that feeds the virus." Tim stopped eating and closed his eyes. He thought for a moment. "We're only like a virus, because we have limited awareness. We aren't true to ourselves." Tim appeared a little surprised at his own conclusion.

Lorraine joined in, still smiling at Doug. "Then that would go with what some people have said, that our ability to understand and think has actually been lowered. We lost our ability to use all of the brain, if you believe those theories."

Margaret said, "Maybe we're being controlled by extraterrestrials. I sort of think so." Her husband glowered at her in shock, his fork poised in midair.

"But the thing that interests me, Tim, just at this moment is maybe that's what we're supposed to discover, that our limitation is not something that is imposed on us from the outside. Maybe it's something inside that we have to discover. Maybe what we're supposed to discover is that the frequency that we are, as you said, Tim, has got to be raised. If that is, in fact, the case, how do we do that? With meditation, with ceremony, with what?" This was a reach for a medical doctor. I was very interested in how far he would go.

"With love," Doug said, leering at Lorraine as she was eating her asparagus one spear at a time.

"It's certainly not intellectual," John said.

"Perhaps it's in your feelings then, in your heart, in your soul," I said.

"I suppose that is how you would approach transition or finding the missing host like a virus does. That's how you manifest change, isn't it?" Tim asked, as he took a bite of honeyed carrots. He knew he had surprised me.

"Basically I think that we are a thought that becomes manifested," I continued. "As you are spiritually, so you become physically."

"If we're looking for the answer—the truth—outside of ourselves, maybe that's the part of our conceptualization that leads to trouble," Ann said.

"Maybe that's what is so out of order, the part that's been troubling me for a really long time. I have been yearning for a sense of wholeness, but I look outside of me into distractions that money can buy. I need to pray and try to find the truth inside my own heart. Does that make any sense?" Margaret asked, placing another helping of asparagus onto her plate.

I looked into Margaret's eyes and smiled.

Doug was now up, wielding his drink in his left hand and walking around in circles, his other arm waving around.

"With the new age, you talk about what's missing. You talk about how you can get better. You talk about the inner baby," Doug slurred.

"The inner baby?" I asked, laughing. "Do you mean the inner child?"

"Yes, one of those," Doug said, continuing. "You talk about shamanism. You talk about Zen Buddhism and becoming one with the universe. All the different things that everybody is teaching. You're looking for what's missing, not realizing, not affirming, that we're already whole. I think we're all just looking for affirmation. At least, I was, and I'm still trying."

"What did Jesus say?" Ron asked.

"One thing Jesus said was that the kingdom of God is within," I said, watching the golden Buddha begin to smile in the subtle candlelight.

"Isn't that really all there is, in a way? Whether it was Jesus or Plato, it was some great philosopher who wrote that centuries ago. And it's the truth. We keep looking outside and taking courses and doing seminars. All that provides wonderful knowledge, but you must realize that you already have everything you need to raise your state of mind," Margaret said.

"My friend, Master Charles, talks about synchronicity. He talks about raising the rate of bliss in your being, which would raise your frequency and kill disease," Lorraine stated as she moved her chair closer to Doug's.

"In other words, you're saying whatever disease exists in your body would all of a sudden have no more food. If you raised your frequency, bodily, it would have to disappear and wash out of the body through the blood," Tim said as the salad was being served.

"Even with true prayer, you would move into a different vibrational field," Lorraine added.

"When you're ill, you know there's something in your point of view that needs to be shifted. So many people are afraid and they stay the same. If you stay looking, you're just looking. So you need to stop looking and you need to shift, but how do you do that? How do you measure yourself so that you don't become static and locked into attitudes that don't serve you?" Tim was asking me.

"You have a yardstick," I said, "a spiritual yardstick, and you test yourself all the time so that you don't become static." The candles were fluttering and burning lower. All the statues surrounding us appeared to be swaying in an ecstatic glow.

"I think you're either growing or you're not—or you're moving backward. Anyone who's stuck, whose feet are in quicksand, dies if they stay there. You have to move on," Margaret said, serving salad onto her plate. She was very pleased with herself.

"But, perhaps, moving on looks different than how we perceived it in the past," Doug said, sitting closer to Lorraine.

"Back to the virus," I said. "Back to this something that has no life of its own. In a sense, thinking that if you were to symbolically draw the conceptualization of looking for God outside yourself, you would produce a force field, a symbol inside you, so to speak, that would have no life of its own. It would hardly have a meaning, would it?" I asked Tim.

"A virus can't live alone, so it keeps searching," Tim said.

"People can feed off money and off other people and dangerous situations and alcohol. But then you're feeding off something else and you're certainly not complete. Like you said, people can behave like viruses," John stated flatly as he buttered a cheese-filled biscuit.

"Isn't there an important key here?" I asked.

"I think Lucifer is about to leave the planet. This thinking something is missing in us becomes something that we have trouble seeing in our hearts, and Lucifer will take us all with him if we don't see this and remember who we are. There's an evilness about this," Margaret said.

"Margaret, for heaven's sake!" her husband sputtered as he took a swig of wine.

"And yet, a virus isn't evil in and of itself," Tim added.

"It's only evil in the sense that we're so ignorant. We're ignorant about our own bliss," I said, going on. "We as a people have this sense that something is missing. There is so much of life that we don't see—our intuition, our ability to love and to heal ourselves. In our stress and confusion, we can feel hollow inside, and we want to fill up the empty places. How about this idea? Perhaps we have created the virus by thinking that something is missing. If we know that we are complete, we create a different energy. Then a virus has nothing to live on."

"Maybe that's what happened when Eve ate from the tree of knowledge. It was the *judgment* of good and evil, not the evil itself that changed everything. Judgment creates duality—good or evil. Depending on how you judge, there is always something missing by implication. Therefore, we bar ourselves from the garden of paradise—a life of health and harmony and everlasting love," Doug said in a moment of clarity. He sounded like the old Doug.

"Love is a powerful thing. But wanting to possess is even more powerful than love, and it will, as Camus said, sterilize the object of your love, because we want to possess it so desperately. Then you possess it and you kill it. You destroy it. You leave your beloved without a face," Margaret said, a bit drunk. Her husband was now really shocked. He had stopped eating altogether.

"We want to possess God in some way. That makes me more powerful than you are. That's part of the new thinking that is kind of tragic. It's like anything else—everybody wants to be the best at what they do, but it becomes a competition, spiritual materialism. I have more miracles. I have more healings. In actuality, the cure for what you feel is missing is all about being humble," Ron said. We were all surprised by his didactic tone and were silent for a beat or two.

"It's funny," I said, "I was afraid to get on that spiritual bandwagon, Ron. For years I just wanted to live simply and write my books and work with my teachers. Then I realized that that isn't fair, because I have been given a gift, and I have many experiences to share. I think that's the only thing I can do. I can write about it. I can teach things. But really, what I'm doing is offering life situations or ceremonies within which people can experience themselves and can experience their love. I realized that I had a destiny to be of service to people, an example, maybe."

"Maybe our problem is that we have so few heroes anymore. People have to look to something to give them the inspiration to move on. Does that make sense?" Lorraine asked.

"Yes," we all agreed.

After a long silence we all sipped some coffee and prepared for dessert—baked Alaska with mounds of white meringue.

"You give hope. You give courage," Tim said softly, as he noticed that I was very exhausted and needed to go home.

TWENTY-ONE

Share What
You Know

A gentle wind blew in off the Pacific Ocean. Katie, one of my closest friends, and I were eating lunch in an old haunt of ours in Malibu. The mountains in back of us were brown and thirsty for rain, and the sun shown relentlessly, sparkling off the surface of the sea. The sound of a gentle surf floated on the wind.

"Katie, I think about faith a lot these days," I said. "I realize that at different times in my life, my faith is challenged as things happen. My old wounds are opened—wounds that stem from lack of self-worth or love or losing youth. When I watch someone dear, like Jim, die in pain, I begin to question the lesson and wonder if the Great Spirit is really there. It's like I'm a trapeze artist who's practiced for years and years to let go of a tiny rod of wood hundreds of feet above the ground, and for one moment I'm suspended in the air, reaching out for the person who is swinging over on his trapeze to catch me. I need extraordinary faith to trust that person is going to be there with his arms extended at just the right moment."

Katie thought about this for a minute before saying, "What I find in my life is that I don't have that kind of faith at all, particularly when it comes to an old wound, and I have to trust someone. Sometimes I can't even trust myself. I'm afraid that I won't even notice if someone is reaching out with hands open, ready to receive me. My lack of faith has always been somehow involved with holding on. I'm afraid I'll fall, so I don't let go of the trapeze in time. Don't you think we hold onto a situation, believing that if we hold on long enough, everything will be okay?" Katie looked glum.

"A kind of strangulation comes from a lack of faith, like trying to hang onto a failing love affair or your old way of life that suited you when you were younger. You hold on tight to something that no longer serves you. You can't get up the ladder of awareness and go from one rung to the next, as my friend Sara O'Meara said, without letting go of the baggage that you're carrying along. You can only go so far, Katie, and then you have to let something go," I said, taking a bite of my BLT and throwing some pieces of crust to the sparrows dancing on the ground.

I felt an overwhelming wave of pain. "I need to let go of sadness," I said. "It seems like I'm going to hold on to that trapeze forever!"

I couldn't help it. I couldn't keep my attention on Katie's words or on my own. My thoughts kept going back to visions of Agnes and me riding through the forests in Canada, along the lakes, or Ruby and me sitting on her porch tying herbs. I'd have flashes of Red Dog or his apprentices, Ben and Drum. Then I would hear the clinking of dishes and silverware, the noise of people talking, eating, bringing me back to the present.

Then I went on, "Jesus said somewhere in the Bible that words have power, and certain words have more power than others. The word of God has power, and it's important for you to keep those words inside you. Carolyn Myss talks about the importance of reading all of the sacred texts. I agree. Read everything that you can get your hands on that has been written with awareness and consciousness. From the Bible to the Koran, all sacred books have sacred words. The word is important. I've written eighteen books, because the sacred word, once heard or read, lives inside you and becomes much more than the word itself. It becomes a picture. It becomes a sound. It becomes a sacred habit."

For a moment my vision blurred, and I saw Ruby talking to me on the porch of her cabin. We were painting a gourd rattle, and she had said to me, "We are in a time when we must share what we know. To hold what we know inside is a refusal to be of service to the one who gave us life. Your intimacy with the Great Spirit is developed through maintaining your dialogue and your service to the Great Spirit. Without that dialogue, there is no intimacy. If you are to be an efficient messenger, you have got to pull yourself together, so that you sit in the center of your circle of truth and access the beauty that is all around you. If you don't take that responsibility, then you are taking a chance of not learning what you came here to learn."

The vision of Ruby faded as I noticed Katie staring at me.

"Hello, Lynn," she laughed.

"I'm sorry," I said, shaking my head. "To me, what's important is to learn how to let go of a situation and trust that it'll be there when I get back, that it's not going anywhere," I said. "What I forget is that if I hang on too tightly, I might lose it forever."

"What a thought," Katie said.

Just then Bruce Willis walked into the restaurant, unshaven, bald, strikingly handsome and charismatic. Suddenly the restaurant was still, not a sound, only the birds chirping. Then everybody was whispering and pointing as if they had just had a vision of God. He came over, threading his way through the tables, and said hello to my friend Katie and gave her a hug, as she introduced me and he shook my hand.

Maybe movies and movie stars are the shamans of our world, I mused, watching him walk away to his booth. There wasn't a person in this restaurant whose consciousness had not been shifted in some way since this star had walked in the door.

"Come on," Katie said, swigging down her coffee. "Let's have some spiritual R-and-R, and go shopping. I need a new T-shirt."

We left the restaurant arm in arm. Thoughts of Ruby kept veering into my consciousness. I knew something was up, and I needed to go see her.

TWENTY-TWO

———

Secrets

It had been weeks since Jim's funeral, and I had spent a long time with Mother and Vanessa until I felt that they were secure before I returned to Arizona. Vanessa had moved in with my mother to their mutual delight and benefit. It was a relief to be home again after such a sad time, but Jim's death and Edna's, too, still weighed upon me. I needed to see my teachers who were staying on the other side of the mountain range, a few hours drive away.

That night we did ceremony, and Agnes and I, Ruby, and Face in the Water talked late into the night.

Without any show of pretense, Agnes's first words the next morning were, "Take a walk, Lynn."

"What? Why?" I managed.

"Someone is waiting for you," she said. "Take the high trail over by the ridge."

She pointed toward Four Peaks. I stared at her questioningly.

"Red Dog," she said, taking a sip of coffee.

After walking for a half an hour or so, I'd almost given up, but he appeared out of nowhere, without warning. He was playing with a rock in his hands, tossing it back and forth, back and forth. He threw the rock to me, and I caught it. My first instinct was to let it drop to the ground, but instead, I held onto it with my left hand. It felt warm and rough to the touch. He smiled at me, but his eyes were cold and severe.

"You're obsessed with me," he said.

I sat back on the sandstone ledge behind me, startled by his abrupt greeting and steeling myself for what I knew would be another psychic battle.

"Obsessed?" I said. I knew he wanted to break me like a brittle twig. I felt the cold and my energy draining out of me as if my blood were water.

He chuckled to himself. "Yes, yes," he said. "You think about it."

"I can't even imagine where you're coming from," I said, but I could feel my will diminishing.

He swaggered like a demonic clown. "Think about your fear. Think about your need for me."

"Need?" I wanted to flee, but I did not. I thought about the rattlesnake, but then put it out of my mind.

"Yes, your need. Everything I throw to you—a stone, a concept—you want to examine it, to feel it, to know its secrets."

I thought to myself about the years that I had known Red Dog, the years that I thought he was dead, and the sadness that had come over me. At first the news of his death brought relief, but then it turned to sadness. I believe I was sad because I had never known him, like the wolf has never known the lamb that he has eaten.

"I was strangely sad when I learned of your death," I admitted.

Why was I admitting this to him? I thought to myself, I have nothing to lose. The more vulnerable I am the safer I am in a warrior's sense.

"Yes," he said, "because without me there's not much sense to all of this." Red Dog opened his arms wide to the sky. "If everything was always good and always light, what fun would it be, and what would you learn?"

"In a way," I said to him, cold in my heart because this man had caused me so much pain, "it's the same for you. Your obsession with the female, your obsession with the power of woman, is only because you can't have her. If you could truly possess her, you could have kept the marriage basket. You could have kept Agnes or the spirit of July in the gourd or the mask of Jaguar Woman. But all you do is captivate. You're like a collector, Red Dog."

"A collector?" he asked.

"Yes. You're like a collector of butterflies. You catch flying flowers that perfume people with light and joy. But your collections don't last long in captivity. I think it's the color and the light, the beauty of a female that interests you. You want to own what you cannot be. You are capable only of being something that is ugly — as if you're stuck in your metamorphosis, squirming around in a dark cocoon. It's you who are obsessed with becoming something more than is possible. You wish to become immortal — that's your obsession."

Red Dog raised his eyebrows but said nothing.

"You're a collector of someone else's creation, someone else's glow. You want to absorb that light until it dies. Then you take your little pins, and pin the soul to the back of a velvet box, and then all you are left with is a memory of the experience. That's all you have, but the memory does not change you. Then you talk about what a beautiful memory it was, all the conflict, all the movement from one poignant reality to another. You are a pathetic collector, Red Dog. I hadn't seen that before. You don't spend money on your objects. You waste time and efficiency and incredible skill in destroying living things by taking hold of them. That's what men and women so often do to each other, though we rarely recognize it!"

Red Dog smiled and turned his rugged features in profile to me. "July wanted your light. She mistook it for love. There was a time when I wanted your light, because you convinced me that you had it, which, of course, you didn't. But you dance and play well through the dimensions. That is your game and your seduction."

"I hope you don't want me now," Red Dog said. He was suddenly very handsome and alluring. "My life is now dedicated to God—God is all there is in my life."

Everything was different from this point on. The whole timbre and feeling and color of our conversation had switched. His body language was suddenly sexy and fluid. The transformation took me by surprise, which is just what he was expecting to do. I began to burn inside like a furnace, until I hurt.

"I have never really gotten over you, Red Dog." Had I really said that? Where did those words come from? I stopped myself. Then I thought, Well, you surprise me, I'll surprise you.

And I had. Red Dog didn't know what to say. He stopped moving and his eyes became vacant and waiting. "That's why you need me," he said, finally.

"No doubt you are celibate," I said, wondering if he was truly a monk.

"Oh, yes, I am celibate and have been for years. I bet you'd like to change that," he said. "I bet you are quite the seductress. You're the Mary Magdalene energy, aren't you?"

"Oh, for God's sake," I couldn't help but say, wondering at this bizarre turn of conversation, wondering if I should run while I still could, before this got out of control. What was he doing? What was I saying? Danger was crawling up my spine.

"I'm playing with you," he said, answering my thoughts. "I'm playing you like a violin. Can't you feel it? Don't you feel more alive? What you never understood is that I have always been allied with the forces of God." Red Dog stood up and moved restlessly around me, back and forth as he spoke.

"You think that God only looks like light, that God can only look one way, that there is no dark side to God." He ran his fingers through his hair. "What you don't understand is that everything is created by God, even the dark. When the dark angels fell or made an agreement to fall out of heaven, I became allied with those dark forces because that is also my agreement with God. I am very old, much older than I appear."

For a moment he caught me. I was confused. Then I realized he was uncertain, too. He was watching me as I closed my eyes. I thought to myself, Yes, everything is created by the Great Spirit. I was unsure what to say or do next, so I simply sat quietly, thinking about his words and my own spontaneous thoughts. I wondered what kind of a trap he was trying to set. His traps meant very little to me, but I still wanted to set a boundary to the conversation, a place where I had control. I needed to have a sense of what he was going to do before he did it, so I was still, because it implied some kind of agreement.

I was amazed to see that he was really that weak, that being right was terribly important to him. My cooperation with him was paramount in this game. He pushed energy out to me, and then he pulled it back to entice me to come toward him. As long as I kept my wits about me, I could move toward him and play his game.

"You manipulate people with your God-given skill. You misuse that power and leave your victims in your wake."

"Ah, but people need to be victims. If they become my victims, it's because they chose that in this life. Doesn't that go along with what you were talking about—mirrors and all that crap?"

"I suppose it does, and maybe you're right in some ways. In part, people do choose their mirrors. There's no question. People do choose to behave a particular way in the world, and they choose mirrors to imprint their spirit shields with experience. But, Red Dog, to manipulate someone for your gain and their harm so that you become more powerful is unforgivable. Perhaps you find that amusing, Red Dog, or naive on my part, but it is a great injustice to those that you meet, and someday you will pay for that."

"Oh, please," he said. "Don't tell me you buy into that. Karma? I suppose that's what you're trying to say to me—karma? I am chalking up bad karma. If you want to talk about controlling people, that's your best example. Listen to me. Bad karma or not, this is a fact. Evil exists in the world. I could turn you around. I could get inside your mind and destroy you right now. But if I did that, then there would be nothing left for me to play with, so I will spare you."

I knew it wouldn't serve me to challenge him. I wondered if perhaps he knew something that I did not, some aspect of this ancient way between good and evil that I had missed. So I shielded myself psychically, hoping that he wouldn't *See* me, but I couldn't tear myself away from him. I had to keep reminding myself of what I had learned in Tibet, that if people *truly* had the power to harm you, that they would never consider hurting another human being.

"Words are magic," he said to me. "Magic words can weave webs of transformation around people."

"Transformation?" I said. "That's not something I'd have imagined you would be very interested in, unless it was good into evil. You are obsessed with control. You want to control even the way people think, the way people dream. Through the magic in your voice and mind, you stole July's spirit and put it in a gourd. She nearly died. What good does it do you to rob other people's power—to control them? That will never feed your spirit. You must have a hole so deep inside you that it can never be filled. What is it, Red Dog, that makes you so angry? What is it?"

"Perhaps I am angry just at having been born," he said in a moment of what may have been the only honest words he ever expressed to me.

From being born? I thought to myself. Yes, it is probably true.

The clouds above threw a great shadow over us, as a cool eddy of north wind danced in circles, raising dust and sand.

"You see, I am not here to take revenge on you, black wolf, not at all." Red Dog pulled his dark coat around his shoulders in an effort to shut out the cold. "I am not here to take anything from you. It's fascinating to me that you absolutely will not hear the truth."

"Your truth is not my truth," I said.

"The truth is the truth," Red Dog said. "Not that you would ever see that. But let it just be said that revenge is not my purpose. Maybe a reckoning. I stole the marriage basket successfully, but you stole it back and returned it to the Sisterhood of the Shields. I lost my female side. Then you kept me from the face of power, the mask of Jaguar Woman. You see, that object could have completed my power. I hated you for that."

I thought for a moment about his belief in objects of power made by others, wondering what he really did with them. I was fascinated by what makes a man like Red Dog continue when there is so little spiritual comfort in his life. One cannot feed spiritual hunger on control or from trying to convince another person to see the world as you do. I never try to control someone or ask them to believe in me or my ideas. I simply share my experience so that they might find their own courage.

"Don't you want to experience some of the great gifts of this life so that you can become closer to the source of creation? Controlling someone is to me a very evil thing. When you look at the atrocities performed throughout human history in the name of God, in the name of religion, why would you ever want to add to this?"

"Because controlling them is interesting," he stated flatly, folding his hands.

"I wonder," I asked Red Dog, "why have you come here now for this kind of reckoning?"

Red Dog waited a long time to answer me. "I have long since given up trying to fill up this hole inside me," he said, watching how startled I was at his candor. "Time, in a sense, means nothing to me. When time stops, I will probably be at peace."

"Time comes alive when the clock is stopped," I said.

We looked at each other, both friend and foe. We had two completely different visions of the world, and yet we walked in the same world. It was as if one aspect of it existed and one did not, depending on who was looking. God has influence in all things. Red Dog once thought that he was exempt from all earthly laws, but I could see he had learned otherwise. And maybe I had learned something about the evil forces in life.

I decided to leave Red Dog and go back to Agnes's cabin. My feelings were so confused. It was a thin line between love and hate. I felt like I was sitting on that edge, looking over the lip of a treacherous canyon thousands of feet below. My memory and my mind seemed to be sliding, like the edge of a canyon falling away beneath my feet, and everything I thought I knew was tumbling down with it.

Tree Blossoms
Fall and the
Leaves Are
Crimson

RED DOG'S BLUES

All my life I command the power
all my brothers

know my soul.

Power divides completely
my way

until now
"at the hour of my death"

singing
an unknown, feminine healing song.

What trickster tricked me back
into this life?

Memory is a bone in the sunset.

TWENTY-THREE

Helpless

Ruby and Agnes sat across from me.

Agnes took off her medicine bag and handed it to me. "Hold this, black wolf, hold it to your heart. Sometimes, Lynn, the innocent one walks into a cruel wind that is not intended for her." Agnes turned sharply to catch my attention. "With your clothes torn from your body, your ears punished by the cold cycle of winter wind and rain, you wait as the mysteries hover over you and glorify you. There is no train that comes this way, day or night, so you must linger until the stillness returns, when the darkness becomes gray. And then you rest."

"Rest?" I managed to ask after the depth of her sudden words unraveled inside me.

"Yes. This is not a trivial time. You are composing the sacred moments of your song."

"I feel helpless," I stuttered, as she reached out to hold my hand.

"My little one," she said, "don't be taken by the beauty of the mountains or the tenderness of truth. It is what you are. Look . . ."

She pointed to the morning light turning the slate-gray sky into blood-red light.

"That's your love," she said. "It illuminates all—the good and the dark—with color and hope. Again, that's what you are. Listen to the angels and the birds in the Tree of Dreams. They answer your call, your longing, to go home."

"It's the spiritual wholeness growing inside me that hurts so much, Agnes. But after all the pain and all the rain, it is my heart that will last forever," I said, drawing a horse in the sand, my tears splashing on my fingers.

"You have a question," Agnes said, taking up a stick lying next to her in the sand. She ran her fingers over its surface, as if she were playing the keys of a piano.

"Well, yes," I finally said. "What did you mean, a wind not intended for me?"

"You are caught in someone else's healing. Your love has created a bridge between you. His healing is a symbol for your own, and it hooks you in a way that is almost unbearable, but it takes you to truth very quickly. You're going through the sound barrier of your soul at the speed of light. And I choose the word *light* carefully," Agnes said. "Light, so quick, hurts the eyes until you're readjusted. So you wait and give yourself time. There are other ways to learn, but you have fallen in love, and the winds of another person's fate are swirling around you."

"Is that bad?" I asked.

"Everything is part of the Great Spirit. Are you learning?"

"Yes."

"Then you are an overwhelming teacher for the one you love, and he for you."

TWENTY-FOUR

Obsession

After meeting with Red Dog and the ladies, I spent a week in quiet, melancholy seclusion back at home. I felt like my heart was broken, and I couldn't understand why. I couldn't possibly be in love with Red Dog, but he presented a face of power and primal intelligence that fascinated me and seemed to obsess me.

I wrote and dreamed, trying to understand what was happening. I do not allow myself the luxury of being victimized, but there were moments when all I wanted to do was relinquish myself to his sorcery. I wanted to give away my spirit to his seductive charm and move softly away from myself. There was trickery and a play of extraordinary passion here. I wanted to let myself fall into that chasm, but surely, if I chose to do that, I would lose my soul. More small deaths, more smoky mirrors hiding the truth. It was all I could do to hold onto what I knew was right for me and stay centered.

Out riding one day, I watched two ravens flying against the

blustering wind rising out of the north. I pulled my jacket tight around me and urged my mare into a canter down the trail toward home. "The cure for all evil is a good canter," Disraeli had said a long time ago. Works just as well now, I thought as I approached my barn, spirits lifted despite the falling rain.

I dismounted and led my horse quickly into the shadowed barn away from the rain and wind. Star nickered softly, and I turned, surprised, to see Agnes sitting cross-legged in the dirt, her back against the wall. She was wrapped in an old Navajo trade blanket. Its red color was startlingly bright in the coming darkness.

"Hi, I didn't see you," I said.

"Sometimes you are blind, black wolf, just like love," the old woman said, smiling.

"Yeah," I nodded. She had voiced the thoughts in my mind. I unsaddled Star and sponged her off, covered her with a blue cooler to dry, and tied her in the stall. Then I sat down near my friend and teacher and handed her a soda from the refrigerator.

"Well?" I asked. "You've come a long way to be sitting here in my barn. What's up?"

Agnes shrugged and smiled, saying nothing. Finally she asked, "Where have you been?" She swigged down some soda.

"Lost in my own emptiness, I guess, floating off the ground and landing hard, only to bounce into the walls. I sleep, ride, talk, rest, pray, and hit bottom, only to see a trail of flowers leading away and away, and of course I follow it. I'm somewhere out there dead, maybe forever, or even worse, perhaps alive forever."

"Don't you know I am looking into your eyes? You think no one is there, but I am here, looking, waiting for you to see me. See me, black wolf, in all of your beauty and your power. You must not give yourself away like this. In the emptiness of space, feel your sister stars around you. They are blessing you and keeping you from harm."

"I don't understand what has happened to me. I feel so much pain. Am I feeling this pain for everyone? I see so much in this life. Lately, it's as if I've been in search of death and have found every possible experience of it. I take death in and ride the hills with that feeling in my chest. Nothing. No use, and then the clouds lift."

"Where have you been?" she asked again.

At moments like these when she confronts me with myself, I stop whatever I'm doing or thinking and wait for an answer to come.

"Agnes, as I looked at Red Dog and felt his seduction and the incredible pull of sexuality that he was putting out toward me, I suddenly saw in the duskiness of the evening the face of my lover, Steve. As you know, this man was a great challenge in my life. He had talked to me in ways that were so alluring he seemed to be from another world. His words were not his. He had no way of understanding through education or experience that what he was saying to me when he talked about God and the forces of light, darkness, and nature was so powerful."

"You have been experiencing such grief. Red Dog has brought this past romance back to you. The loss has magnified. Go on," Agnes said.

"My lover Steve surrounded me in a passionate cocoon that became a straitjacket for me because I lost myself in it. As if bewitched, I so completely surrendered to him that I didn't know who I was anymore. I felt a passion with him that I had never before felt. I saw his face in Red Dog's, fleetingly, but it was there, Agnes. Red Dog had been working through Steve. He had taken my energy by tapping into my ability to love. He had played with me in the most evil of ways, taking my heart and throwing it around like a ball. There was such joy, laughter, and pain. I would have done anything for him. I was beyond reason, beyond my own power. I left my creativity and my responsibilities behind. I have never done that before or since, Agnes."

Agnes watched me, nodding or shaking her head occasionally at my words. Finally, taking a deep breath, she reached out her hand and touched me.

"You have great protection around your heart, Lynn. But is it not true that the area around your heart was constricting you? Did you not suddenly develop asthma—asthma that you do not normally have? It felt like asthma, didn't it?"

"Yes," I said. "Yes, that's right, it did."

"The constriction you felt in your lungs and around your heart was a manifestation of your guardians. They were protecting your heart, but they had to work so hard that it felt like strings of wire."

Agnes placed her hand over my heart, then she reached up behind me and placed her other hand on my back behind my heart.

"So tell me more," Agnes said with a mysterious look on her face.

"I have tried to put that relationship out of my mind," I said, "because I knew toward the end that it was all wrong. I knew toward the end that there was something more to this relationship than what I could see. With all that I know, I could not penetrate what was happening to me. I felt a kind of possession. I would go about my life, but I was only partially there, because I always had him in my mind. And he would play with my thinking constantly. We would talk on the phone and he would twist me around. We would be together and it would be highly sensual, highly sexual, as if he were taking that energy from me and using it for his own power. I know now that he didn't really have the skill to do such a thing. I didn't know at the time that Red Dog was after me, too. He learned a lot about me through that relationship. He learned about my strengths and my capacity for love. He played with me until there was very little left of me for him to steal.

"At that point I recognized it so deeply that I began to pull away. But he performed an unbelievable dance of seduction and I could not free myself. My energy had dropped so low that he even decided to let me go, so that he could come in again when the energy had been restored. And when I had wrestled my mind back from the sleep it seemed to be in, he, like Red Dog, decided that he would be celibate, that our relationship could not be based on a physical attraction. Of course, our relationship was much more than this. The physical attraction was only a result of the incredible magnetism that was between us. But we ended so abruptly that I feel sure that Red Dog must have had a hand in our demise. He had worked through my loved one and other people in my life as well. And then he had left us alone for awhile. He had left us alone until I ran into Red Dog himself. The way Red Dog moves, the way he dances—as if he's suddenly hearing music in his mind—he is like this man with whom I was so in love. There is no question that he has been after me for a very long time. I thank the Great Spirit that I know it now, and I'll never let it happen again. Never, Agnes, never."

Agnes looked at me sternly. I remembered when I had first met Agnes and Ruby, Red Dog was very seductive at that time also. I had become obsessed with him long before I knew much about the ways of power. I remembered a night when Agnes had actually tied me to the bed to keep me from leaving the cabin.

"Agnes, I felt at the time with this man that my spirit had been captured. I was unable to perform the magic and the mystery that I know I am capable of to free myself from this kind of attraction."

As I finished speaking, Agnes pushed on my heart from the front. Then she hit my back with so much power that I felt as if a bolt of lightning had exploded in my head and traveled through my body. I passed out on the floor of the barn.

When I awoke, it was dark outside and Agnes had covered me with a horse blanket. I knew she had fed the horses, because I heard their contented chewing in the background. It was a sound I had always loved. I took a deep breath and reached out to Agnes, feeling strengthened and relieved.

I took her hand. "I'm here, wise one, I'm here now."

We walked together to my house and ate quickly before going to bed. The next morning we left for her camp before dawn.

I turned to my teacher as I threw supplies into the back of the truck. "Sometimes, Agnes, I simply want to lie down, enveloped in the energy field of the Great Spirit, close my eyes, and listen to his beating heart. I want to feel that sense of oneness with the universe that surrounds me with such joy and purity of power. I understand that as human beings we want something greater than ourselves to be our God, our power. I realize very clearly that the kingdom of the Great Spirit is within me, it's within you, Agnes, and all of us. Inside. We go up to the top of a tree to see a view out across the landscape. And that's what it is—a view across the landscape, isn't it? It doesn't help us get closer to the sky fathers any more than digging a hole gets us closer to mother earth. The ability to climb up the tree of life, our Tree of Dreams, is inside us all the time, isn't it?"

Agnes nodded to me and put an arm around my shoulders as we got into the truck. We were on our way back to her camp. I was beginning to feel better.

"There was a time," she said, "when I thought there was no Great Spirit, and I laughed at people who told me that there was. I had lost my husband in a logging accident just a short time after our daughter had been taken by the dogs in the middle of winter. She had crawled out from our tent and gotten attacked by the dogs before we could get to her, and she was lost to us. I didn't care about God or anything resembling the Great Spirit. It was then that I learned my greatest lessons," she said as we headed out toward the mountains. "I went to a shaman woman in the Sisterhood. I was called to them, and I learned about the weavings of magic. I learned about many things to do with the mysteries of this life. It wasn't until then, you must understand, that I realized that I had to go inside myself to find the answers and just stay alive. Of course, at that time I didn't care if I stayed alive. Without the Great Spirit, there was nothing. Without my husband and my child, I thought there was nothing. But I realized they lived on inside me, as Jim and Edna live on inside of you, Lynn. I can see them through your eyes."

"Yes," I said, "I see that now. I do. I see it clearly. It's when I think too much and try to explain the mysteries of life that I get lost. That's when I get in trouble every time. You know, Red Dog did me a great service by approaching me in the way he did. He appears to be talking about spirit, but what he's discussing is the mind, the ego, and the frailties that live within so many of us. He makes me face my fear of death, my own mortality."

"How does he do that?" Agnes asked as we bounced down the road rutted from the rain.

"I've been so afraid of him all these years. He makes me, or I make myself, walk into the center of my fear. He also attracts me; like my father, he is brilliant and yet abusive—my age-old lesson."

"Yes," Agnes smiled.

At the bottom of my sadness, a small light was beginning to burn, and silhouetted there was my secret treasure, my joy. The sun had begun to rise over the horizon behind the mountains. Pockets of black shadows, elongated reflections of the clouds drifting above, were now turning to crimson edged in gold.

I finally said to Agnes after many silent miles, "The Great

Spirit created such beauty for us. I think, Agnes, we create that beauty too, because we are part of that glorious light in the sky. I see us there on the edges of those clouds with golden, shimmering beauty."

I turned left onto the dirt road leading to camp.

TWENTY-FIVE

Eagles to Crows

"It's not necessary for eagles to become crows. That's what Cochise said. I think it was Cochise," Agnes said, sipping coffee with me. We sat on the portal of the cabin and watched the desert come alive with the morning sun.

I thought about her words. Crows are carrion birds and they feed off dead things. Eagles, however, kill and eat only live prey.

Ruby had joined us and then Face in the Water as well. They sat around me. As they had done when we first sat together in circle, Face in the Water placed her palm over my hand and held it there for quite some time, letting me feel her strength, helping me to center.

"What is it?" Face in the Water asked me.

"For many nights I went to sleep thinking that maybe there was no Great Spirit, there was no God, because fate seems so cruel and because of these discussions that I have had with Red Dog. Suddenly, the meaning of life as I knew it is very different than I'd imagined. I sense a hierarchy of control and manipulation. My thoughts feel paranoid, so very different from anything that I would ordinarily examine."

"You're not a Pollyanna, as you would say it," Face in the Water giggled, "but you see the bright side of the mountain. You tend not to walk on the dark side of the mountain, even though those trails are necessary to get to the top. You have learned this in your work with Sin Corazón, our only sister to be pulled away by a sorcerer and returned later on, and now in your work with Red Dog."

"Work?" I said.

"Yes, work," she said.

"But I don't understand. Why has Red Dog come back to bother me?"

"Ah," Ruby smiled. "So he has touched a nerve, has he?"

"Yes, Ruby, he's touched a nerve, and it is of great concern to me, because when I work with people, I see their fear. I see their worry about the evil in the world. There is God, but why is there so much pain just to teach us? Why does that have to happen?"

My teachers were sympathetic, but I could see them smiling at my predicament just the same.

Agnes, her smile flashing bright, saw my confusion and read my thoughts, as she always does. She said, "You don't listen. Sometimes you don't listen. You don't hear the words of transformation. You yourself teach this, little wolf. There are words and experiences that do not originate from your personality, or even from this lifetime. Those words are created by the magic of alchemy and the energies that are brought together to transform. These energies exist to teach us."

"Ah, Agnes, yes, to teach us. But why must the path be so painful? How can that be correct? How can that be part of what is necessary?"

Face in the Water joined in. "You are seeing the illusion, Lynn.

You are believing the illusion. Our time here on Earth is a part of the dream, part of the sacred dream. But it is an illusion."

"It's not an illusion when somebody pinches me and it hurts." Ruby shook her head.

"Little wolf, Red Dog is a skilled sorcerer. He has gotten inside your head and turned you around, just like he said he would do. But you're smarter than that. You're so much smarter than that."

And suddenly, as if to illustrate her point, Ruby, with her mirrorlike eyes and uncanny strength in every muscle in her body, grabbed the low-hanging branch of an old Lepo pine and clambered, literally, up into the tree. I hadn't realized it, but Twin Dreamers was also up in the tree, where she often perched to dream. She crouched there like a buzzard, her hair loosely falling around her face—her old, extraordinary face with young eyes looking down at me and laughing.

"Okay, okay," I said, "I get it. I'm not supposed to take myself so seriously, right? How could I, with both of you hanging like a couple of old bats in a tree? But this is serious," I said to them. "This is something that I see as demonic, because it challenges my belief in what's holy in life, and that's almost never happened to me, ever. Somehow Red Dog has managed to reflect some hidden aspect of myself that still lacks faith. How could I have been unaware of that? More than anything, it's my ignorance that disturbs me."

Ruby was now balancing on one of the highest branches in the tree, moving up toward Twin Dreamers.

"Look down," she told Twin Dreamers. "What do you see?"

"Well, I see Lynn worrying about evil. I see Agnes and Face in the Water trying to urge Lynn, with their intent, to see that everything is created by the Great Spirit, and we are part of all that," she said very seriously as the treetop began to sway perilously down toward us.

I repeated her words a couple of times in my mind.

"Then what you are saying is that we all have some of that darkness."

"You see," Ruby interrupted, "we are looking down at you struggling with light and dark and what you think about this and what you feel about that, just as the Great Spirit looks down on all of us as we agonize through our lives, trying to make the right decisions, this and that and the other. Does it really make any difference? Probably not! Hopefully, our decisions support the light. But if you were the Great Spirit and you wanted to teach these human beings about consciousness, what would you do? Would you have everything made of light or would you find someone to agree to represent darkness for all these people?"

"Well, maybe so," I answered, watching them at the top of the Lepo pine thirty feet in the air. Ruby and Twin Dreamers had shifted their weight and the treetop began to sway and dance in the wind.

She yelled back down at me, "Don't you see what you have to do?"

"No," I said, "I don't. I don't see what I have to do. I wish I could change it all."

"Ah, what a good idea," Ruby said. "Let's go and see if we can change God and do a better job."

I looked up at her, not knowing what to say. They had each lived through terrible times, terrible injustices, and yet their acceptance of all things was remarkable—remarkable and infuriating. I just wanted to scream. So I sat down in the dirt, but instead of screaming I started to laugh. Laughter bubbled up from deep inside me, and I was overcome by the hysterical humor of it all, looking up at those two old wild women in the tree, as agile as children, looking down at me.

"Well, little wolf, I think we'd better dream on this. What

do you think I'm doing up in this tree anyway?" Ruby started giggling.

"Yeah, me too," Twin Dreamers said, teetering on a branch.

Now we were all laughing, shrieking, guffawing and giggling hysterically.

"Actually, I can't imagine what you're doing up there. It doesn't look very comfortable to me," I said between shrieks of laughter.

"It's a heck of a lot more comfortable than being down there worrying about the forces of good and evil," Ruby laughed.

Agnes jabbed me in the ribs.

"Get it?" she said, snickering.

"Get what?" I asked, shaking my head, unable to stop laughing.

"Don't you see, Lynn, it's more of the divine play. Maybe the dark forces agreed to be dark for the Great Spirit, so we would have the opportunity to actually learn something. Maybe it's true — that part of what Red Dog said."

The desert around us echoed with our voices. We laughed and spoke words of teaching that curled around the incessant laughter that seemed to have possessed us all.

"But the part that is not true is that you must get caught in the dream. Don't forget that — there's no need to get caught in the dream."

"But these past few months have been all too real," I said. "It's as real as bleeding to death or agonizing over your children that have been shot in front of you. Those things may be part of illusion, but try telling that to the people who are living through it."

"Yes, they are painful, horrible things, but they don't have to put an end to all light," Ruby said. "As human beings we have got to learn somehow. How would you suggest that we learn?"

"We should go to school," I said.

"Yeah, right," Agnes said. "Right. I think a lot can be learned in school, as long as you have beings of light around you, so that they can perceive what can't be taught and what isn't written, so that faith can grow in their hearts. Yes, sure, school is fabulous. School can help us learn many basic lessons, but the ABCs are not going to teach you about good and evil. Only the Great Spirit is going to teach you about good and evil."

"And the Great Spirit has given you a great lesson," Ruby yelled from the top of the tree, "a great lesson. You go and you think about it, black wolf. This is your time."

"I still don't understand what you're doing up in that tree."

"From up here, maybe we represent a different level of consciousness," Twin Dreamers said. "Maybe we represent a higher level of consciousness that we're all moving to, or the inside of the circle of consciousness, closest to the source. We're looking down at you, listening to all of this talk."

"Blah-blah, blah, blah, blah," Ruby said.

"Oh, for heaven's sake. You mean to say that I need to move my consciousness up and climb a tree for perspective?" I was laughing and yelling and getting hoarse. "Is that what you're saying? If I see it in perspective, then I'll see that life is magical and even an old shaman woman can climb to the top of a pine tree."

Then, as if a lens opened within my memory, light came through. I felt blinded for a second, and then the sensation passed. I could see that Ruby had reached out her fingers to me. I felt as if she had hit me with a thunder bolt. For a moment, I could see, truly see, what she meant. Evil could indeed be a part of the light.

At that moment, Ruby and Twin Dreamers started to climb down from the tree. I noticed that they were wearing gloves. So, they had planned this. The Lepo pine was rough and sappy, I'm sure, under their hands, but they came down that tree with enormous skill. They shimmied down the tree and landed safely on the ground. I couldn't have climbed to the first branch. Thank heaven they hadn't asked me to climb up there with them. We all ended up rolling around, laughing until finally catching our breath, and lying in the sand, we came back to ordinary consciousness.

"Okay, I'm starving," Ruby said.

"What's for dinner?" Twin Dreamers asked.

"Well, you finally got it," Ruby said. "Quite honestly, it was a beautiful view from up there. Maybe next time I'll ask you to bring my dinner up to me. That's the least you could do," she said, winking at me. We all sauntered off arm in arm toward camp.

TWENTY-SIX

Circle of
Agreement

Weeks later, I returned to Agnes's hogan to find Agnes and Ruby, Twin Dreamers and July. I was thrilled to see July. I hadn't known that she had been there for almost a week. July had brought me a medicine bundle for my stepfather's passing. We laughed and hugged, ate quesadillas with little strips of nopalitos, and talked about all the things that were happening in our lives. I love these women so much! As I looked at the four of us, I giggled to myself. How different a circle this was from my friends in Los Angeles!

"I heard about Red Dog," July said, traces of fear in her eyes. "Are you okay?" She reached out to me and held my hand.

"Yes," I said, though not absolutely sure. "I'll tell you about it later. I don't want to think about him now. This is your time. It's not often that we initiate someone into the Sisterhood of the Shields."

July was a bright and welcome presence. She is a young woman now and has chosen not to have children. She talked about her life in northern Canada and how much she enjoyed it and how very happy she was to now be where it was warm. She has a beautiful face with shining eyes and beautiful teeth when she smiles. She wore shorts and a T-shirt and sandals. Her hair hung long, down her back, glistening black. She had grown up.

Twin Dreamers looked like some kind of divine native street person. She wore intricate jewelry made out of silver and colored beads. Her dress was sewn with tiny mirrors and colors of red, yellow, and black. Her face was old and creased or clear and unwrinkled, depending on how the light reflected. She laughed. Her hair was wild and unkempt and pieces of grass and twigs were woven into it, yet she was fastidious.

I relaxed, finally, in their company—this society of women who had become a family to me. They had helped me so much with my sadness, the difficult transitions that had shaken my foundation over the last several months.

But I knew there was work to be done today. This was a very important time for July and we needed to prepare her. I glanced at Ruby, catching her eye, and we both rose together.

Ruby grabbed July and said, "Excuse us, ladies. We need to go for a walk."

The next thing I knew we were following a deer track down into a dry wash. We walked quickly, following Ruby's deft steps through a thicket of prickly-pear cactus. A cactus spine ripped into July's arm as we swung around a curve in the deer track, and she yelped in pain, stopping to pull out the spine that had embedded itself.

"What is the devil?" I asked, turning my body toward her in silhouette to the sun. July's cheekbones shone gold in the shadows of her dark young face. She wore a bone necklace and had tied her long hair back with a silver barrette.

"Something or someone that pokes you and makes you hurt," she said, half kidding, as she threw the spine away.

"Don't you take me seriously?" I asked.

"No," she said, then looking at my stern demeanor, said quickly, "Yes, of course I do."

"Well, then?"

"The devil, I would say, is real if you entertain that reality."

I turned and went on down the narrow trail. My moccasined feet made no sound, unlike Ruby, who shuffled along, sending up puffs of dirt and dust that billowed around her feet.

"The devil will take me when I die, the devil will take me when I die," she sang in a mocking tone.

"If you don't express your intuitional nature, you create negative thought forms," July said.

"Blah, blah, blah, blah," said Ruby, tripping on a rock and creating a large dust cloud that I breathed in and coughed out.

Ruby and I, without another word, sat down on the trail on either side of July.

"Sit," I said, handing July my buck knife.

"Dig," Ruby ordered, placing her palms on the ground.

"Here?" July asked, as we stared at her. July shut her eyes to center herself. Ruby startled July by whispering in her ear.

"Dig, July, dig. Dig down into the earth as if searching your soul. Dig deep where the spirit comes from, where your soul emerges from the heart of mother earth. Find that sudden spring sparkling like mica in the moonlight. Go to your source where the seeds of winter become spring flowers."

July began to dig. The ground was hard and unforgiving. She wasn't thrilled with this project. First, she pointed the knife into the ground and immediately struck a rock. She tried to push the blade around the rock, but to no avail. Ruby and I sat with arms crossed, looking at her expectantly. July couldn't get more than a half-inch into the ground. Finally, she sat still, wondering what to do next.

After some time she said, "My soul is probably just as hard

to fathom." Then she remembered her water canteen. Pouring a large circle of water onto the ground, she waited a moment for it to soak in and dug her knife into the soil, dislodging the rock with one swipe.

"Yeah!" she whooped.

"Your faith and trust is like that water," I said, pinching the wet sand with my fingers. "It helps you go deeper into your spirit more easily. Just as the water loosened the sand, trust that the Great Spirit helps you to find your way through the darkness."

After a few minutes, Ruby started to giggle, reaching her hands over and covering them with more water from her canteen, wet dirt, and sand. She leaped toward July like a frog on its hind legs and smeared her face with dirt. Then I did the same. July bolted upward only to be caught and rolled over in the wet sand and dust by the two of us. At first, July was yelling, and then all three of us were rolling around, laughing hysterically and completely filthy. Finally, July sat up in disbelief. We were sitting in the middle of a deer trail like three mudlarks as a buck and two does watched us in equal amazement.

"Have faith, July, but don't believe in anything too rigidly," I said.

"Don't try," Ruby said. "You'll only get in the way of the Great Spirit."

"Just be," July said.

"Yes," I nodded toward the deer, "like them, but we're in their way. Now they have to walk around us. That's how your energy works when you try too hard—it has to take a different trail. Do that too often and you get weak, because your power source is diverted. That's when the devil comes, because your weakness feeds the devil. Sometimes your weakness feels like love, but in truth, it can kill you or the one you love most."

"Loving or the devil?" July asked.

"Both—because you can love someone to death from your weakness or your beliefs. The devil, however, takes form only when you take him seriously." I stood and gave July a hand up. "You did well, July. You held your intent but changed your method."

"And you didn't get too glum," Ruby added. "Lucky for us!" We laughed as we walked way off the trail and the deer bounded by.

Ruby grabbed July's hand and stopped her. "Stay playful, July. Never, never too serious."

In a sense, I envy July's young position in learning. As I look back at those wonderful early days when Agnes and Ruby were teaching me, I sometimes see pictures inside myself like Picasso paintings, all bright shades and squares of light.

Crimson, Gold, and Orange . . . the Leaves Begin to Fall

Words breathe
and the truth shatters illusions.
Mind shatters darkness, shatters red-tailed hawk

flying now. I knew Lynn's mother
and her father, Jim.

Singing in praise and thanks for what has come before.
Time, no time,

the breath
between winds.

TWENTY-SEVEN

Panning for Gold

I visited Agnes again a few weeks later. After working at home and writing, I desperately needed a break.

Face in the Water decided one morning that we should walk up a tributary of a small creek about an hour's drive away in northern Arizona. It had been raining and the desert floor was pungent with the scent of new flowers. The cacti were almost bursting with an overflow of water. The clouds were black above us, but the sun shone in wide glowing shafts of vivid yellow light that were strong and beautiful. There was a gentle breeze from the west and it was cool.

We wore high river boots, as we had been fishing downstream. Leaving our fishing poles behind, we were now walking through the water the best we could. Large rocks, granite outcroppings, blocked our path. We climbed carefully, the stones slick with newly nourished lichen. Because of the rain, the water was quite high, but as we rounded a corner in the stream, the water suddenly seemed shallower and quieter.

Up ahead I heard a noise. Face in the Water seemed to ignore it. I looked up, wondering if perhaps there were deer coming down for water. As we went around another turn, I saw the back of a woman. Much to my astonishment, when she turned to look toward us, I saw that it was Ruby.

"Ruby," I called, "what are you doing here?"

"You should know," she called back.

We walked forward. The sand beneath our feet seemed firm. There were fewer rocks and boulders at this point. The stream spread out and was shallower than it had been before. Ruby stood up and we saw she was turning a large round pan in the water. She lifted it, still turning and turning, and sand and water spilled over the lip. She shook it gently and turned it more.

"Drat," she said, as she stepped in a low place and the water spilled out of the pan.

"What are you doing, panning for gold?" I asked.

"Well, yes, isn't that what you do?" Ruby retorted.

"What in the world are you doing out here panning for gold? Are you that hard up for money?" I couldn't believe it and started to laugh. "This takes the cake," I told Face in the Water. She laughed and shook her head.

Then Ruby sat down on a large outcropping of rock and dangled her feet in the water. She put the pan back in the water and down into the sand. She lifted it up, turning it and turning it. Water slowly spilled out as she jiggled it back and forth. I sat down next to Ruby, and Face in the Water sat on the other side of her.

"You see, the gold is always heavier," she said to me.

"Oh," I said, "so you allow the sand to spill over with the water?"

"Yes, see those little glittery pieces down there?"

"Now how can you see that, Ruby? This is ridiculous. You're totally blind."

She laughed at me and continued to pan for gold as if she could see perfectly. She held the palm of her hand over the pan at one point and could sense either the power or the vibration. She could read something in the gold by the palm of her hand.

"Here, you take this. You're the one that's so good at this," Ruby said.

"I've never done this," I replied.

"Well, you're good at finding gold in people. You found us, didn't you?" she said.

"Yes, but it wasn't exactly a gold mine," I laughed.

Ruby poked me in the ribs with her elbow. "Come on, you try it."

I dipped the pan into the water and down below the sand, pulled it up carefully, yet still spilled sand out into the stream. "I'm obviously not doing this right," I said.

"Well, you're supposed to be very careful so that the gold doesn't slip out with the water and the sand." Ruby had a sneaky glint in her eye. She craned her neck around, watching me as I turned the pan, and said, "Hmm, well?" I kept turning the pan. "That's fool's gold, isn't it?" she asked. I was looking at little glittery pieces of shiny yellow gold. "Well, see if it sinks to the bottom," she said. I turned and turned.

Face in the Water sat with her arms folded and her eyes closed. Perhaps she was taking a quick catnap, I thought. As I spilled the water over the edge of the pan, the little pieces of gold went with it, floating right to the top.

"Oh, it was fool's gold," I said.

Laughing, Ruby said, "Ah, yes, maybe that's what you need to-day—more fool's gold."

"Oh, Ruby, I'm not in the mood," I said, feeling disconnected and frustrated.

"What's wrong, little wolf? You're not in the mood to learn something about your enlightenment?"

I stared at her while holding the pan and dragging it across the bottom of the creek. Coming up again, I carefully swished the water out until the sand settled to the bottom.

"I don't know, Ruby. I'm just in a funny place today."

"Oh really? For the first time, I suppose," she said sarcastically.

"Ruby, I think it is the first time I've hit this plateau."

"It's a plateau of what?" Ruby said. "I'd like you to describe it to me very carefully." She put her finger to her cheek.

"Well, I'll answer your question, even if you don't want to hear it. I don't really care."

"Oh, please," Ruby replied. "Aren't we a little uppity today."

"I feel uppity. You're darn right. I feel frustrated, because I can't quite understand what I'm going through. Actually, I don't even know if I'm going through anything. Maybe that's what's the matter with me. I'm not going through anything. I'm dull," I said, as Ruby laughed.

I heard something to my right and looked over to see Face in the Water snickering with her eyes still closed. Just what I need, a couple of old Indian women making fun of me, I thought. I took a deep breath.

"All right. Frustrated, disturbed. Disturbed, that's what it is. Disturbed!"

"Huh, you must be in love," Ruby said. "You must be in love."

"I may be in love, because I so passionately don't want to die. I want to feel life—painful or not."

"You're in love, because when you're in love, you're disturbed. Or you're at peace, which means love. Love, the way you think about it, in love, means that you find your source somewhere else besides inside you and the Great Spirit. And when you do that, when you move outside of your center in such a way, then you feel disturbed. Nothing is quite right, is it, little one, little wolf?" she asked.

Then Face in the Water opened her eyes. I turned, feeling the force of her, and scrutinized her face. Her eyes were crystal clear and shining like the water that I held in my pan, with flecks of gold like the sand settling to the bottom. She said, "See? Blindly in love. It's a big one for you, black wolf. It's a big one. If you figure this one out, I'll give you a gold nugget!"

Ruby and Face in the Water laughed and laughed.

Then Face in the Water watched me with concern.

"Why are you looking at me that way, Face in the Water?" I asked.

"We have spoken a great deal about vulnerability and how vulnerability can be your greatest shield."

Ruby splashed the water with her pan.

"Vulnerability can be a skill," Face in the Water continued. "When you are digging or panning for gold, your vulnerability is one of the greatest skills you can have."

"How do you mean?"

Ruby added, "When you're with Red Dog and act like a know-it-all."

"I never act like a know-it-all," I interrupted.

"No, you don't. And for the most part that is to your credit," Ruby admitted. "When you are working with Red Dog and he begins to talk to you in some way about what he knows, you have a quality," Ruby said, while smoothing the sand that she had now brought up from the creek. Tiny flecks of light were in the pan, gold reflecting from the sun. "You see, little wolf, you have this skill to sit back inside your own consciousness. You create a void. People misunderstand that void and think that you don't know anything. But you know a lot. You know everything, in a sense."

I looked at her with surprise.

"Don't be shocked. Strangely enough," Ruby taunted me, "I do know who you are. Of course, I taught you everything you know."

"Yes, Ruby, I do know that." I nodded and smiled toward Face in the Water.

"When you go into that void," Ruby continued, "you move away from your consciousness and into second attention. Most people don't understand second attention. They don't even know what that means. What I mean by that, of course, is your place of kinship with spirit. You move into that place where the power animals roam. You see that devil, that dark sorcerer, who is trying to keep you from the top of the mountain, when in fact, you are always in a position of learning, whether you are me or you, little wolf. You know that; you know how to listen.

"You know how to pan for gold. You observe a person, listen deeply, then jiggle that pan, and you wait for the sand to settle and the water to clear. You watch that, symbolically, in other people. You talk to the gas station attendant. You talk to the guy in the hardware store. You talk to the person who fixes your car. And you ask questions while moving into that place of the void instantly. You know that everyone has gold inside them—a spark of light—if you can just find it."

"You carry it with sacredness," Face in the Water said, "and you know, Lynn, you don't do this to make a fool out of anyone."

"No, I don't," I said.

"You do this because you know that the Great Spirit lives in everything and everyone," Face in the Water continued, "and there's gold in all of life and in each of us."

Ruby cleared her throat. "Ahem," she said, now holding the pan on her knees. She twisted it around a few times and ran her hand over the top of the water as if she were honoring it in some way. Her hair was loose, which was unusual. It floated on the breath of wind as though the Great Spirit was speaking to her. Wisdom shone through her blind eyes into mine as she turned her head to look at me.

Ruby spoke on. "You see, if you could teach your apprentices to simply be unassuming of their knowledge, then they can learn and work. And yet, the ego moves into the place of love and kicks love out. That sorcerer tries to keep you from the top of the mountain. That sorcerer is the ego, always and at last, the position of fear. It inspires fear, that sorcerer. It tries to make you afraid of going any further. If you get twisted up in the drama that people create, you get lost in a darkness. And heaven knows, you lose that vulnerability, that place of opening where you can help someone."

"Can you explain that further?" I asked.

"Yes. You inspire their greatness. You know that inside every person is an oracle. Perhaps you want to learn something on a given day. Maybe you're out in the middle of the desert. You don't have your teachers around. You have only someone checking groceries in a grocery store, let's say. You go in, you talk to them. You ask them a question that comes to you from your body-mind, from your spirit. That evokes a response. They may not even know what they are saying. But the Great Spirit speaks to you through them, through their knowledge, that perhaps they don't even know they're in touch with. It changes them. It gives them something, and it gives you a magic moment that enters you and brings you light."

That night, exhausted, I fell asleep in my hammock. A dream came to me.

I climbed down a ladder leading into an underground cave or kiva. Tied bundles of herbs, drums, and painted prayer sticks hung from wooden trellises at one end of the round earthen room. I saw a quick movement in the shadows and then Spider Woman appeared, dressed in black velvet, her large silver earrings shining against her tanned face.

"You can't be whole without the feminine," she said.

"Is that the key to Red Dog?" I asked in my dreaming.

"He's on the dark side of the rainbow, Lynn, because I gave him the song of life. But I have also taken his memory away. He cannot remember it, so he has come back for you."

"But I don't have the song. That's not my medicine," I said.

"But you have the power of relationship. Let us all desire this one end and find love within each other. The song is a gift from the feminine realm. How could he have had the song and not want to own it?"

"I am learning about my weakness in love," I said. "I am struggling, Grandmother," I added.

"Soon you will transform out of your mind and move purely into heart. He is teaching you without knowing it. He wants one more chance to find the song. He sees it in you."

Spider Woman tossed something into the air, and suddenly a great burst of white light filled my eyes and the kiva. I blinked over and over, trying to regain my vision. As I opened my eyes and looked up, I saw Spider Woman standing, holding a lightning bolt in her left hand—her body was only a skeleton.

"Spider Woman!" I cried out.

"Be still. Look at me," she said. "Am I not a shaman woman who causes the thunder to roll and the lightning to strike? Like you, I cause the wind to blow and the song of life to be sung."

The room began to tremble, pieces of dirt falling from the ceiling. I could hear the wind blowing as I continued to stare at Spider Woman, who was slowly taking her form back. I felt honored and joyous.

"Don't you want to sing?" she asked me. Once more I saw her throw something dusty into the air, and a burst of light filled the room again.

"Listen and sing," she ordered.

I had to sing. The sounds of music fell from my tongue. I heard a beautiful song, melodious and haunting. I was singing a language I didn't understand. The aches in my body went away, my heart felt clean and strong, and my mind seemed bright and open. I felt rejuvenated and filled with love.

"Red spiders run in the deserts and a great mist is growing and coming forth to surround you. Your message is a tricky one, but I think you are ready now."

The song faded along with my own words echoing in the night.

"I've heard the song, I've heard it, Spider Woman. Thank you."

The sky was black and the stars were bright. Again, I fell into a deep and dreamless sleep.

TWENTY-EIGHT

A Cave
of Stars

I woke early in the morning in Agnes's cabin. The morning air was still. Large ravens had settled in the trees shading the cabin and were calling loudly to each other. If they were trying to awaken me, they had succeeded. It must have been no later than five-thirty in the morning, and I could remember only fragments of my dream. But I felt instantly alert, as if I had slept out in the wild and heard that rattlesnake again. I looked around and saw that Agnes, Ruby, and Twin Dreamers were all sleeping.

I quickly put on my clothes and walked outside, shutting the door behind me very quietly. I looked around and to my surprise there was a ground fog, a cloud lying on the earth, reminding me of my dream, saguaros peeking up through the very top. The cloud was so thick that I could barely see the desert floor except in certain places. The ravens cawed loudly and flew away, disappearing into the grayness. I started to walk down toward the creek, the fog

dense and heavy around my legs. I wanted to swim on the clouds.
The fog was impenetrable.

I walked a few steps and stopped. My senses were highly at-
tuned. I felt the back of my neck tensing, rippling with fear as if I
were in imminent danger. My body became alert and ready. I
picked up a walking stick that I had laid against a tree. I had
worked on this walking stick for years. It was made from a piece of
alder wood that someone had given me long ago. It was strong and
hard and long. I poked ahead of me in the fog, feeling my way instinctively, because I had walked this trail down to the creek hundreds of times. I had the sense that I might walk off the edge of the
earth. Fog is so uncommon here and I had never seen anything
quite like it in the desert. This was something that would happen in
the tundra of northern Canada and other places that I had lived. I
knew something unusual was about to happen. Thoughts raced
through my mind. Was it a puma? Was it something hungry and
dangerous?

I heard a branch crack, and I crouched down and whirled around
at the same time. There was a hill off to my left, and there I saw him.
My heart was pounding. Red Dog stood in the fog like a slender
ghost from another time. He wore his vestments, long black skirt-
like material that floated up around him. He looked in his stance as
though he was no longer a friend, no longer someone who wanted
to talk, to converse, to exchange ideas. He looked like he meant me
great harm. I stayed low to the ground and simply stared at him.

Then he reached out his hand and said, "Come," his words
floating over the fog. "Come."

I didn't move. I didn't know quite what to do, but I sensed danger, so I wasn't going anywhere. He began to move, starting to
walk down from the hill. Then he took a turn in the trail and
walked behind a saguaro and disappeared.

I sat there not knowing whether to follow him. I was at a crossroads of power. One instinct was to go get Agnes, but I thought, No, this isn't about Agnes. This is about me and Red Dog. So I stood up, feeling him tugging on my luminous fibers. I thought to myself, Was that his double? Was he showing himself to me in spirit, or was he really there? It didn't matter. He was equally as dangerous. Then I thought, I've walked into danger before. I guess I'll walk into it again.

I walked up the trail, around the saguaro, and waited there, looking through the layers of fog, trying to see him. The fog had lifted above the crevice that the creek created in the rocks. He was seated on a rock down by the creek.

"Come," he invited me.

I walked down, open and aware, and I went to sit across from him.

"Why are you here in our camp?" I asked him.

"What better place to be?" he replied. "Are you afraid?"

"Why would I be?" I asked. "But I know you like to win. Winning and taking someone's power is everything to you, is it not?"

"Why, Lynn, that is beneath you. That is not true," he said.

I studied him, trying to see him through all of his disguises.

"Come on, Red Dog, cut the crap."

He was irritated with me now, acting as if I had completely missed the point.

"I realize, Red Dog, that we can talk about life and death so easily. If somebody were to hear this conversation, I'm sure they would think that it was absurd, and in a sense it is. However, you and I deal with life and death every day. That's the nature, I believe, of enlightenment on this plane. I look at you, and I see someone who lives in the world of darkness. Yet darkness is a companion to light. Somewhere you communicate and cross those boundaries. You make choices all the time, to stay in the light or in the dark.

"Why would we want to hurt each other? Why would I steal from you, if you haven't taken something that belongs to me? I'm not going to steal power from you. What I'd like to know is why would you steal power from me? Why would you want to take something that doesn't belong to you, that you haven't even earned?"

"Ah," Red Dog said. "But if I can take it from you, then I have earned it, because you haven't done your homework, and you don't know how to hold your power. So it belongs to anybody, and I may as well take it."

After a long pause, Red Dog stood up and paced back and forth in front of me. "Interesting energy, isn't it?" Red Dog said. He reached up his hands as if he were stroking the air. Then, he looked me up and down from head to toe. Slowly, with deliberate movements, he unbuttoned his vestments and let them fall to the ground.

"What are you doing?" I asked, shocked at his alluring and yet powerfully still demeanor. He wore jeans and a simple white long-sleeved shirt.

I stood there staring into his eyes, taken by them. I knew I was protected, but I felt suddenly tender and sweet. Yet something like a far memory way back in my heart was tugging at me. I thought my heart would burst with delight. The secret did not belong to me, it belonged to Red Dog. I saw the comfort and seclusion of it was what he had been hiding behind. It was his altar, the dark side of the altar behind which he felt great safety and power. I could see it.

"You have a secret, Red Dog," I said barely able to speak.

"Yes, and I want to share it with you. Come with me. We can dream together. The universe of stars awaits us. Let's feed the craving of our dream. Let's fly together as we were meant to be."

I stepped backward, placing my foot on the side of a stone, and slipped, falling backward onto the sandstone ledge. Red Dog kneeled in front of me and began massaging my twisted ankle and my calf. I knew he was trying to shift my attention into dreaming, because his strongest allies were there. I wanted to spread my wings and fly away with him.

Then suddenly, my consciousness came crashing back. I had willingly walked halfway through the turquoise gateway with him. Could I have ever come back? I didn't know, but it was doubtful. It's akin to that moment just before you tread over into insanity. There is a moment when you can pull yourself back. If you don't, you can create energy triangles in your mind that plague you forever.

I wanted to fall prey to him. I wanted to discover what he knew, what it felt like to wrap a blanket of darkness around me. I wanted to allow him to come closer and become one with me. For a moment, it was all I wanted in the world. I noticed that the fog was getting more dense and darkness was closing in around us.

Then without warning, a shaft of morning sunlight penetrated the grayness. I heard a clap of thunder and the blistering of lightning in my head. I thought to myself, What in the world am I saying and doing?

Red Dog was still massaging my calf. I realized I had been quiet for a long time. I had been entering the dream, some kind of strange fog. It had felt oddly safe and seductive. I thought for a moment that Red Dog and I could actually join together.

"I'm sorry for trying to hurt you," he said.

"I see stars in the earth, in the cliffs behind you," I said.

"Stars," he whispered.

"Yes," I said, seeing a small cave in the rocks. We sat outside the mouth of the cave and spoke about his god and my sense of spirit and death. Then he lifted me gently with his arms and said, "I have something to show you." His touch electrified me.

We entered the cave, and out of the darkness came tiny sparkles of light, pinpoints that shone like new pennies in the sun. I was hypnotized. Then the darkness seemed to envelope us—a magic moment, a magic cave. We floated on the darkness for a long time, holding each other softly. Then the starlight shifted and went away, and there was nothing.

Before I knew it, we were sitting outside again. The whole day had passed, but I knew as we watched the sun setting over the mountains that dying was like returning to the stars from whence we came.

"We exchange our light and become simply a different form of that light as we shift into a new consciousness," Red Dog said, reading my mind, his cheek close to mine and scented faintly with cedar. "Maybe you saw your own death in the stars," he continued, picking up a smooth rock. He looked into my eyes and began rubbing the rock with his thumb.

When Red Dog moves into his second attention, his place of *Seeing*, he uses a stone like this. I watched him intently as his consciousness began to recede away from me. I desperately wanted to follow him. Often when I would sit in the sand at the ocean, I would watch and feel the tides changing and pulling back from me.

"It's like life force," he said, sharing my thoughts. "Eventually it recedes from us, but in doing so, like the ocean, it simply returns into the greater sea of consciousness, the greater oceans of water."

Red Dog was not leaving me. He was simply using his skills to lift his frequency into a more elevated and pure state where I would be comfortable. In this state he became The One Who Sees. He could see me as I truly am—my wellness, my connection to power.

"Spirit always takes care of us," Red Dog said. "Even in the soul of darkness, goodness can happen if you receive it momentarily as a teacher. But remember, it is important to see mirrors in everyday things. Your greatest learning can come from anyone. The Great

Spirit will employ even a difficult person, like me, to teach you. Or maybe I have found different messages on the winds and I'm beginning to grow."

"I don't trust you for myself," I said. "But I want to."

The wind picked up from the north, bringing a cool relief from the heat. I could see Red Dog was beginning to come back to me. We sat in silence for a long time. His eyes were slightly open now, looking far off into the distance where dreams are born. I was in awe of the power we shared, the beauty, the tenderness, as he gently held my face in his hands. He caressed my neck and my hair and then touched his lips to mine. I wanted to kiss him forever.

In the middle of my reverie, a brilliant beam of light came shining into my face. I saw wolf spirits everywhere, my guardian animals, circling me and viciously alert. I knew instantly that everything I had just experienced with Red Dog was a terrible lie. I was in great danger. My alpha she-wolf was about to rip out my throat if I didn't pay attention. I looked into her eyes; she looked into mine. And with a jolt my soul came back from the dream.

The vision of my wolves left me as fast as they had appeared, but I knew my power animal was still looking through my eyes at Red Dog. Dogs don't like wolves. They are afraid of them.

Red Dog lurched backward as if I'd hit him. He scrambled up to a standing position. He knew that his trickery and deception was over. "I didn't really want you," he said, his face turning dark and ugly. "You always play the fool, but I know where you're at and I know your power. And someday, I will have it, along with your soul!"

Just then the wolves came back out of the fog. They were in spirit, but Red Dog could see them. They began to tear at him. He grabbed his vestments to beat them away, but they began to devour him and chased him off into the fog. That quickly, he was gone.

I was left there with the brilliant sunlight streaming down

around me. I sat, crying tears of sudden loneliness and evaporating terror. The sun was warm and soothed my aching heart. The seduction was over. My heart began to beat normally for the first time in weeks. The scent of silver sage came up on the wind, and I breathed deeply, knowing that I was safe for a while. I got up slowly and looked for the cave of stars, but it was gone too.

When I returned to the cabin, the women were sitting out on the portal. They came to meet me, knowing instinctively what had happened. They touched me all over, as if looking for some physical wounds. My ankle was beginning to swell, but otherwise I was not hurt. I began to tell them what had happened, and they listened wordlessly, as shaman women do. They laid down several blankets on the portal. I curled up with my back against the cabin wall.

Agnes placed her hand over my heart and whispered to me. "People should not be afraid of death—we experience the growth it brings so many times in our life. When you are afraid, as you were of Red Dog, your spirit disconnects until you start to love yourself again. It's love that conquers death and fear."

I smiled and fell into a deep sleep.

TWENTY-NINE

Holding Power

Agnes and I sat by a dirt trail watching a deer scampering through the underbrush. We were waiting for July, who was coming back from visiting her grandmother in Tuscon.

"It's unusual for a deer to be out during the day, isn't it?" I said to Agnes.

"Yes, she must be very thirsty," Agnes replied.

It was a little doe, probably two years old, very sweet and not very frightened of us.

"I have felt many small deaths in my life, Agnes. One of them was with Red Dog the other day. I felt as if a grayness was entering into me. For a moment, when I was speaking with him, it was as if my consciousness went away and his consciousness entered mine. It was also a great magical journey—it was so hard to come back."

"I know," Agnes nodded.

A big grackle flew into the palo verde tree above us, squawking.

We must have been near her nest. She was very disturbed. She flew away after a few moments, making great commotion.

"Well," Agnes said, "many deaths—we have spoken of this often. It's like being with someone that you give your power to, even when you wish not to, when you feel lesser, and when you compare yourself. Many years ago we talked about the difficulties of comparing yourself. Never compare yourself to another person. It's an impossibility, and yet, we do it day in and day out. When we reach the age of wise blood, the sacred gateway into the second half of our lives, as we call it, we forget the fact that there is no second half of our lives."

A warm wind lifted the corners of Agnes's scarf, and I took a deep breath, breathing in the scent of desert foliage.

"You see, there is no beginning of life and no end of life. It's just an agreement that we make when we come onto this earthwalk to experience the mirrors of aging, the mirrors of different seasons of life," Agnes said. "But it is a dream, and it is an illusion."

"I know that, Agnes, and truly, even before I knew you, I felt that. My family didn't think in those terms. They knew that they were getting older, but it wasn't a big topic of conversation like it is today. We just stayed healthy, it seemed. So I didn't feel that small death until Jim passed away so suddenly. And then it was a huge death."

"It's a death," Agnes said, reaching over and touching my shoulder with her palm and very gently holding it there. Looking into my eyes with what seemed like flashes of lightning, Agnes said, "You have not resolved your grief, and it separates you from many of the joyous experiences that you could be having. That grief shadows you," she said after a moment.

I looked down at the ground, tears filling my eyes. "Yes," I said, "it seems a shadow. And yet I can feel my stepfather shaking his head and saying, 'Please remember me and the happinesses and the joys that we shared. Please remember me with goodness in your heart. Don't remember me with sadness.' I feel that, and then I feel guilty. Damn," I said, striking the earth with my fist. "Damn."

Agnes closed her eyes, and then I did as well. "Think of the worst that you could think of," Agnes said. "Think of the grief. Where is it in your body, Lynn?"

"I feel it in my solar plexus where I'm shielding myself from pain. I feel it in my heart, like it could break."

"Go into that place of broken heart," Agnes said. "What do you see?"

"I see tears and sheets of pain."

"What do those sheets look like? Become them," she said.

I imagined I was a sheet of pain, and I looked like a wall of flowing tears. Waterfalls of pain took away all my other feelings. Only the pain remained. I allowed this vision to envelope me for several minutes, and as I did so, the desert grew silent, and the wind blew up from the west. The scent of sage accompanied each breath. I felt the pain come over me in waves. I sat there, completely engulfed in my thoughts and in the pain, beginning to think it would never leave me. Eventually the water began to turn from slate gray into sparkling water shining from the sun. And as I tried again to find the pain, it seemed to have just gone away. I breathed deeply, and Agnes placed the back of her hand on my cheek.

"Open your eyes, little one," she said. "Maybe the pain never completely goes away. I still remember my husband. I still remember my little daughter, wondering what she would be like now if she were still alive. But I know that she is alive, and I know that she is around me and is in a better place where she is needed. I will see her again, just as you will see your stepfather.

"But do not carry the pain, because it holds you back. The pain that you transfer and project onto other things does not need to cripple you. Pull those projections back. Pull them back," she said, closing her eyes, and now placing the palm of her hand over my power center while pushing gently. "Hold your power, Lynn. Hold your power. Do not give it away to others."

Just then, over a small hill and around the corner came an old pickup truck, red, bleached from the sun. One fender was missing over the left front wheel. Bouncing down the hill came July, being driven by Twin Dreamers. That in itself was enough to make me pause. Twin Dreamers driving. They bounced along with a cloud of dust and stopped in front of us.

July leaped out of the cab, the door grinding and squeaking open. She ran around the front of the truck to give me a big hug.

"July, we're glad you're back. It's so wonderful to see you again," I said. We were all excited as we piled in the truck and drove back toward camp.

"July, I'll never forget those days, long ago, when I was wandering through the wilderness, trying to find Agnes's cabin," I said.

"Oh boy, I'll never forget those days either," July replied. "That Red Dog had stolen my spirit and put it in a gourd."

"It's hard to believe, looking at you now, that Red Dog once stole your spirit and you were close to death. What an extraordinary experience that must have been for you!"

"Ah," Agnes interrupted, "remember when I was talking to you earlier about giving your spirit away? You have to want to give your spirit away before a sorcerer can take it from you."

"That really happened to you," Ruby said. "You must always remember the danger you were in."

July was Ruby's apprentice and there was no question of that, ever, even though I worked with her, also. Ruby always sat off to the left of July, and I always had a sense of her being in an elevated position in relation to July, even though they may have been sitting on the same flat ground. July had great respect for her teachers. She would never second-guess us. She might ask questions, but if it was firm, there was never an argument. She would never dishonor her teachers. July's reverence seemed almost to crackle in the air. July had absorbed deeply Ruby's teachings, so deeply in fact that something was happening that I had not known about.

"I am beginning to lose my eyesight," July said. My mouth fell open as I stared back at her beautiful brown eyes filled with such light and clarity. I didn't know what to say. I thought maybe she was joking, but as I watched her and listened to the silence that suddenly enveloped us, I realized that she was quite serious. I looked to Ruby for some sort of explanation, but she said nothing.

Face in the Water came out of the hogan with Twin Dreamers. "Gee, what's going on? You all look terrified," she said.

July started to respond, "I must be . . ." but then stopped talking for a moment. Finally she asked, "Was it something I said?"

She sat down, realizing that this was a rather serious silence. There we were, old friends finally gathered together after having been apart for quite a few weeks. The sun filtered through the branches of the trees and the shade of the portal. It was so beautiful, I wanted to cry—my friends, my teachers, July being here. We had shared so much. Everything from northern Canada to the Yucatán to Australia together, each experience bringing us closer together.

I stood and walked to where July was sitting, and peered into her eyes, looking for an injury or some sort of explanation.

"When you say vision, are you referring to your eyesight?" I asked.

"Yes, I am. I am losing my eyesight," July replied.

Ruby sighed loudly. I was dumbfounded and searched Ruby's face, trying to read her thoughts.

But July had clearly come to some conclusions on her own. "I think that I have become so much a part of my teacher that in order to learn and to grow, I am willing to endure a loss of vision, as my teacher has," she said.

"But Ruby was blinded," Twin Dreamers said. "She was blinded by surveyors, by their compasses, after they raped her when she was very young. That cannot be the same thing, July. Is it?"

"I don't know," July said, "but I know that I love my teacher so much that I will do anything to learn the lessons that she has to teach me—even lose my vision."

Suddenly, Ruby reared up off her chair and twirled around toward her student.

"Yes, July, you speak the truth. And while it is true that you are my apprentice, we each are different, one from another. If your eyesight does not reverse and become better after our ceremony tonight, then we will have nothing more to do with one another."

Her words were so sharp, sudden, and direct that we were shocked into absolute silence.

Tears began to course down July's face. "Ruby, how can you say that? I honor you with all that I am."

"Nuh," Ruby said. "You do not honor me. You honor yourself. And you will not become as I am. You will become the best of what you are. My blindness is not yours. You do not need to learn from my blindness, except the error of your ways." Ruby glared at her apprentice, took her by the arm like a child that had been naughty, and led her from the portal.

We all sat in helpless silence, in circle, wondering what to do next.

"Well," Agnes said, "just like Ruby to ruin a perfectly good afternoon."

We laughed weakly, knowing that we were faced with quite a drama, wishing that it had happened later, when we had had a chance to put our arms around July and love her before such a difficulty would descend upon us. Still, we all knew that this is the way it was and always is in life. It seems to be, these days, that our teachings are swift and irrevocable and often almost deadly. We talked for a while, comforted by each other and the knowledge that ceremony was being prepared for that evening. So we fasted and then went off to rest.

All the Leaves

Have Fallen

and the Trees

Begin Their

Winter Dreams

The poem
leads us
into the old songs.

Once, the chant
signified pure rhythm,
the soul open

to the inside fire,
the forgotten mind,
the waiting action.

Who steadies
the hand

steadies the mind.
Out in the cold —
who has not been there?

Singing the poem, the poem,
and the old chants in the night in the rain.

THIRTY

Spiritual Family

That night, as the sun was setting behind the mountains, we entered the circle to do ceremony. July seemed visibly shaken by what had happened earlier. We said nothing to her or to one another, but moved deeply into our own place of sacredness.

We smoked our ceremonial pipe, passing it sunwise around the circle, saying prayers to the Great Spirit, to mother earth, to our ancestors, and to all those who loved us. Then we passed the talking stick, a magical ceremonial object that had been lovingly decorated with carvings, paintings, and feathers. Ruby held the precious stick, and she asked for all of us to love each other. She talked about spirit and the power found in the unity of all life. She passed the talking stick to me, and I asked for clarity. As the stick made its way around the circle, the sky became very dark. We settled into the comfort and shadows of the night. The sky was elegantly dark, like black satin with stars shining like painted designs on a ceremonial ghost shirt. It was beautiful and deep, the richest sky I had seen in a very long time. The moon had not risen yet, and it was as if all the lights in the world had been turned off and we could see the stars for the first time.

I knew teaching would soon come upon us, drawn from within us and from the wisdom of Ruby and July.

As I held the talking stick, I said, "I celebrate all of you as my sisters. I thank you for asking me to be part of this circle. I am humbled by the position that I sit in. No matter what transpires with us, I know that we have, in our own and separate ways, grown even more toward elderhood and wisdom. And yet, I feel the primal beginnings of mother earth inside me, as if I am a volcano about to erupt, making new forms and new surfaces that will reflect even more of the light of the Great Spirit. My heart is full, and I feel so joyous in your presence. I feel only the willingness to allow something new to enter that, perhaps, has not ever occurred to me before this moment."

I looked across the circle at Twin Dreamers. Her eyes were kind but always a little fierce and wild at the same time. She might be capable of absolutely anything at any given moment. For now, she seemed content to sit with us in circle, quietly, but I felt an electricity in the air.

She took the talking stick and looked at me. "Your people have lost so much."

"What do you mean?" I asked.

"You have lost your spiritual families, your community," she said. "We in the Sisterhood share this wordlessly, from heart to heart and from soul to soul. There is a communion between us." We all nodded our heads in agreement. "There is a communion beyond what I know and see in your world. We are in a new way of being. We are becoming visible in the world for the first time through your work, through your books, through your school and your efforts with people. So I want to put out a request for a new story."

Twin Dreamers took a crystal, and reaching out, she placed it in the center of the circle. I could see that it reflected a strong beam of light into each of our eyes, and it forced me to blink.

"This crystal represents a dream. It's my dream for the future, which, of course, is the present." She laughed as only she can laugh.

There were twigs and little pieces of grass in her hair. She is a living animated art form. She is a consummate shape shifter so completely different from the rest of us. She teaches by shifting the actual image of herself into something that will elicit change in you. She will become a terrifying monster or an eagle or a laughing old woman in a tree. She is a Kuna Indian from Panama. She has tattooing on her forehead in shades of red and black. She is precious to me.

"I see a dream for your people, black wolf," she said, her eyes glittering, not unlike the timber wolves that I have seen. "The dream that I see for your people is to find a circle of life that honors your elders, something that your people have forgotten. I know that you spend a great deal of time in life trying to encourage the growth of this concept with our sister, Face in the Water. I'm going to place this dream in the center of this circle, and we will make it so. I make this bid for power."

All of us nodded in agreement. Tears were running down her face and her cheeks. I had never seen Twin Dreamers with so much intensity behind her words. Again, the light from the crystal blinded me for a second, and I thought I saw Jim emblazoned in the glow of light. A collage of pictures, retirement homes, old people in wheelchairs staring at white walls. And for a moment I saw the rain forests in Central America and Twin Dreamers and her elders going into the forest to pray, but all the trees had been cut down and their lives were changed forever.

I heard myself saying to Twin Dreamers, "We will heal all this."

Then my vision was pulled back without warning, and the light was gone.

Now Face in the Water rose, backed away into the shadows, and came back toward us. The drumming in our circle sounded like hundreds of drums. Some sounded as if they were coming from far away. I watched as her silhouette disappeared into the shadows and returned almost immediately. She was in the form of her double, as a power animal, the great condor. The moon, which had now begun to rise, shone behind her, a wind was swaying through the trees, and she became an awesome dark silhouette, with her wings spread out, moving toward July. She held corn in her talons. July was suddenly terrified by the appearance of Face in the Water. I don't believe she had ever seen her in her bird form. Face in the Water spoke directly to July and grabbed her with her beak, leading her around the circle. Ruby also walked around the ceremonial circle, singing, and holding an abalone shell and fanning sage smoke with her storm eagle fan.

Face in the Water dropped July in front of Ruby and said, "July, you must taste of the world. Eat up this world—both darkness and light. As you taste, the outer vision becomes insight. Your vision will come from within."

With that, she thrust the corn into July's hands. "Taste this corn, the corn that represents the harvest of all that you have accomplished. It represents the fertility of your spirit. It is from the sacred void of mother earth. You carry that void, and all is born from you."

July was frightened, but began to lift the corn to her mouth.

Something had happened within the circle. There were clouds of smoke around us from the copal and sage we burned. I couldn't see what was happening, but the vortex of energy was moving in a circle with such strength, I wondered if I was going to be lifted off the ground. I became dizzy and images closed in on me and then moved far away. The smoke obscured my sisters from view, but I was in a reverie, unable to distinguish the movement around me.

Suddenly, my consciousness snapped back to the ceremony, and there was a shriek from Face in the Water. Between the swirling smoke, I was horrified to see that her giant beak was tearing July's eyes out. There was no blood and July seemed to suffer no pain. July appeared to offer her eyes to Ruby, who held them like precious stones before placing them inside her own eyes. She sang a sacred song as she did this, and then, with great care, she returned them to July.

Face in the Water was twirling around, as if dancing on July's head, creating a great forceful wind that drove sand into golden waves around us and swirled through the trees. She was an angry whirlwind, but this was Face in the Water as she embodied her animal spirit, the carrion bird. With her extraordinary power, she can digest all poison and transform it back into life.

Then just as quickly as she had appeared, she was gone. July was sitting in a trance but seemed whole and unharmed. I saw that she had eaten much of the corn. In my utter amazement at having witnessed this transformation, I stood up and crossed the circle to July. I could no longer tell what was driving me or why my attention had momentarily shifted. I picked up the corn from her hands, which meant by sacred law that I would then be initiating July into the Sisterhood of the Shields. With Edna's death, there was a place for someone new to enter.

I went back to the center of the circle and sat holding the corn. As quickly as she had appeared in her animal form, I noticed Face in the Water was now sitting as if nothing had happened, on the outside of the circle. As she joined us, I went back to the outside next to her, holding the power of the west direction.

Now the howling of a hundred coyotes split the air, howling and screaming and crying and yipping. It made the hair on the back of my neck stand up. We all whirled around, searching the darkness. I realized that Agnes had disappeared and off to our left came a coyote as big as a wolf. She sat holding her head up to the sky, howling and howling. In the background the multitude answered her back. It was thrilling. It was a primal call, and in my heart I knew it was a call for all of the universe to wake up and witness this ceremony. All of the winged ones, the four-leggeds, the two-leggeds. All of the beings on this planet were to take heed. Again, she howled.

Then, looking to the other side of the camp circle and the ceremony, I kept trying to clear my vision, wondering if I could trust my eyes. There was Red Dog standing in his black robes like a vampire. He perched above us on a high tumble of boulders and I thought I could see his feet and hands become paws with sharp claws, and his face elongated into a toothy grin.

The wind swirled around us and carried thick, lavender-colored smoke, a mixture of sage and copal. I could see that Ruby had lit more copal, but it burst into smoke and cinders and flame. I wondered what in the world was happening now, as my wonder turned to fear. What was Red Dog doing here? The women knew of his presence but did nothing. Was there some reason they didn't ask him to leave? Is this what he had been waiting for—a sacred ceremony where he could impose his darkness into our light once and for all? The pungent odor of the copal made me heady and dizzy again. Was it the clearing out of psychic debris? Was it the strength of the copal that caused me nearly to lose consciousness next to the fire?

Suddenly I felt Spider Woman behind me.

"Wolf-self, make yourself present and seen. We need you, now, in the west." She thumped me on my back, and as a moment of doubt entered my mind, she thumped me again. Without question, I began to take the form of my great wolf. Not wanting to take my eyes off Red Dog, I looked back up and saw him still standing there, snarling, but he hadn't moved. I realized that he didn't dare. He might present himself, but he wasn't going anywhere.

Suddenly there was a high-pitched whistle, a sound so piercing that everything seemed to stand still in the warm, heavy air. A great elk galloped into the circle. I had not seen Agnes take her form like this in a long time. We were a council of power animals surrounding July. The elk whistled again and came up to July, speaking to her words that I could not hear. July slowly stood up in front of this magnificent elk—so beautiful, shiny, and powerfully muscled. I knew now that July's initiation was going to take place. A rebirth would occur from the death we had witnessed in July.

Ruby, still in her human form, stood up tall and blindfolded July. She led her counterclockwise around the circle, speaking in her native tongue. Then Ruby spoke to us all, over the center of our circle.

"Come from the distant mountains. Come from the hills in which you live. Come to the center of our circle, great eagles of the sacred fire. Great beings of our universe and of the Sisterhood of the Shields, please enter, now."

One by one the women of the Sisterhood of the Shields appeared—Zoila, Spider Woman, Ani from Nepal, Ginevee from Australia. A wind came up around us as Edna as She Who Walks with the Wind in her spirit form appeared around the circle with all of the other women. José, Zoila's husband, was there in his doubling form, standing behind Zoila in respect for this circle of women.

Then, Sin Corazón, who was dressed in a black skirt and blouse with a silver concho belt, her long, silken black hair braided down her back, awesome in her power, joined us. As she came over to July, reaching out her hands, I knew that Sin Corazón was in her real form, not her double. She came to July, and then she came to me and took the corn that now lay at my wolfen feet. She picked it up and took it back to July along with a rolled-up red blanket that Ruby handed to her. Inside that blanket was our sacred bundle, our pipe, and many items that had been added to this bundle over centuries, things that will always be secret and known only to us.

An hour of ceremony went on as the women from all over the world arrived, one by one, ghostlike figures in their doubling. Some were in their real figures, some in their power-animal figures. It was a council of extraordinary power. Pieces of tiny mirrors were sewn into their shawls and long skirts. They wore turquoise, coral, silver, and gold. They carried drums and beaded feathers. These women are elders, and they are luminous from the wisdom they have gained through the centuries of their lifetimes.

Then their various shields began to spin like flying saucers through the sky. They emerged, as if from out of the earth, and stood, as the women put them on tripods to be presented to all of us. They were beautiful, glistening in vibrant colors, with feathers that hung from the rims and fluttered in the night air.

Fires had been lit because the air was cooler now. A wind had come up from the north, the place of spirit. We took up our drums and began playing. We started to dance around the fire, disappearing and reappearing from the trailing copal smoke that floated above the earth.

July, who was still blindfolded, was now receiving a beautiful red, black, and white blanket from Spider Woman, who placed it around her shoulders. Then I sat across from July with the sacred pipe. Ruby was sitting next to me, and I was asked to do the pipe ceremony for her. I held up the pipe to the Great Spirit in our ceremonial way. July placed the corn in front of me, as it represented the harvesting of our ideas, the harvesting of the effort, and the joy and pain that July had been through in her life.

All of the women began chanting and drumming along with the

sounds of calling birds and the howling coyotes and wolves. It was a cacophony of sound beyond my imagining, and rich in meaning and detail. The power of the ceremony was breathtaking, and it was difficult to keep my consciousness together. Certainly it was beyond description for anyone else's believing, and yet the beauty of this ceremony had to be told. The power of ceremony inspires us to realize that there is more to this world than what we normally see. It was magical, and I was standing in the middle of the miracle of magic. Even as I marveled at the wonder of my experience, I remembered Red Dog still looking down upon us.

Ruby's voice brought me back as she spoke to July. "You must search for your eyes," she said. "Your vision is an inward process, my apprentice. It is not just an outward seeing. You have witnessed so much with us. You have found power, but also you have lost your own spirit and soul to Red Dog, who even now is here with us. He still holds that empty gourd. If only he could find you or another to fill it with power so that he could be whole. But never will it happen again to you, July. You are free of him, because you *See*. You have found your juggler eyes. You have found the eyes that were lost to you. You were going to give them to me, but I will not receive them and neither will any other living person, because you have found your true vision. Your life belongs to the Great Spirit first. The gifts that the Great Spirit has given to you belong to you to cherish, not to destroy. It is forbidden by spirit.

"So, let Lynn take off your blindfold, young one, and join our circle of women for forever. It is law, and it has always been this way. You are one of us. You are part of the Sisterhood of the Shields."

As I untied her blindfold, July's eyes shocked me, for they glistened and reflected like mirrors. She Who Walks with the Wind circled July, honoring her, and giving July her place in the circle as a sister of light. She briefly looked over at me and smiled, her spirit self glowing, and then faded away. I cried with joy for seeing my old friend. Then she was gone.

Sin Corazón came over to July, dancing like the black panther, moving in and out of her animal self, sleek and black. She leapt from one rock to another, watching Red Dog seductively as she did so. Then she prowled around July, as if they were exchanging their power in a dance of shamanic joy.

July began to turn and swivel around in the sand with her arms outstretched. She turned and turned, as if she had become the center of a whirlwind. She began to chant in her native tongue, beautiful and deep. Slowly, she became her power animal, the wolverine—sleek and strong, a fierce warrior to the end. The wolverine is a powerful being unknown and unfamiliar to many of us because she is from the north. Her wolverine nature was close to me, and never having seen her in this particular form, I realized why we had always been so close. We were four-leggeds together in our packs, teaching our young how to live and how to hunt, teaching others what we know, so that their lives can become more full and more beautiful.

"I have my vision. I have my eyes," July said. "I own my vision forever. I understand that you are my teacher, Ruby Plenty Chiefs, but I also understand that I am alone. I am alone in my learning and in my teaching. You are part of me, and I am part of you, but we stand separately. I take my power on my own. My truth, the divinity of all that lives, is within all of us. I celebrate my initiation with the gratefulness of my heart and my spirit, forever." She began to dance. She moved in and out of her form, for she now possessed the skills of the Sisterhood.

Then we all danced. What a sight we must have been—chanting, drumming, and dancing. And on the hill was Red Dog, in his darkness with his empty gourd that had once held July's spirit. But her spirit did not belong to him, and as I watched, he left the gourd behind on the rocks above us. He seemed to shrivel away into nothingness and disappear, because no man could be present here now. Only the Sisterhood, forty-four in number, continued with the ceremony for several hours. Much of this ceremony I cannot share, but I will say that its magical quality was unparalleled in anything that I have ever seen.

As the sun began to come up over Four Peaks, their jagged silhouette glowing purple and orange in the sunrise, Agnes came across the sacred circle to me. We were no longer in our power-animal forms, and she handed me the ceremonial bundle.

"Soon we will all go and feast, but remember, Lynn, that there is no ending to this ceremony or to your book. This is only the beginning. The story never ends," she said, hugging me warmly.

Epilogue

There is magic in this world if you want the world to be magical. If you want life to be special, it will be. No one wants to be bored or consumed by ordinary drudgery. But what happens, all too often, is that when magic is presented to us, we don't believe it because we don't trust ourselves. We don't realize what can really be accomplished. We don't realize that if we wish to, we can take other forms. We can sit in the presence of the great masters, angels, or ancient seers of wisdom and find peace and wisdom, but it takes many small deaths, the giving away of old limitations, to get there.

I want you to know that there is much, much more to your life than what you think is there. It doesn't matter what you believe in—which god, which life, which creator, which messiah. It doesn't matter. What matters is your ability to love. What matters is your dialogue with the divine and how you manifest that in life for the simple joy of it, for the healing of it, and for the inspiration of beauty that it provides for all those around you.

ENTER A COSMOLOGY OF MYSTERY, MAGIC AND
POWER WITH LYNN ANDREWS . . .

"For more than two decades I have been describing my learning and my path.
It has been a joy to do this. In continuing my journey, I would be grateful if
you would share your insights with me.

"You are also invited to join me at my annual spring retreat for four days
of ceremony, sacred community, meditation and healing. In addition, ex-
panded in-depth training is available through the Lynn Andrews Center for
Sacred Arts and Training, a home-study course beginning each February.
Please call or write for schedule dates and detailed information."

In Spirit,
Lynn Andrews

Please send Lynn your name and address so she
can share any new information with you:

Lynn Andrews
2934½ Beverly Glen Circle
Box 378
Los Angeles, CA 90077
(800) 726–0082
Website: www.lynnandrews.com

Meditation

Anthony.
3 bottles 104.90. 3 bot.
2 bo
anch. top —

Physical, Mental, Emotional, Spiritual

Love = compair wish x-mass
Look for the source of your power within

1-800-230-0776

19.95.
Bob Barefoot. coral calcium

Kevin Trudea
TV. Program Debbie + Kevin

3 books + 19.95. (moth sapn)